COLLECTOR'S EDITION

Entertainment WEEKLY

THE ULTIMATE GUIDE TO

Supernatural

PHOTOGRAPH BY MATTHIAS CLAMER

Contents

PHOTOGRAPH BY MATTHIAS CLAMER

ON THE SET WITH S.E. HINTON

The author of *The Outsiders*, a *Supernatural* superfan, remembers the first time she met Sam and Dean—and Baby.

WHEN I STEPPED OUT FROM THE TRANSPORtation van into the bright Vancouver sunlight, I squealed like a fangirl at the sight of the Impala. I kept shaking myself, unable to believe I was really here. In Canada. Visiting the set of *Supernatural*.

And it had all started with my first and only fan letter.

As *Supernatural* was beginning its third season, I decided to write to Eric Kripke, the showrunner of the television series that had captured my imagination. I tried hard to make my letter a good one. I detailed what I loved about the show. The subject: I have always been interested in the paranormal. The relationships: My books have always been about how people

S.E. Hinton shares a few photos from her visits on-set. Clockwise from opposite left: Abaddon (Alaina Huffman) peers out from a window; Hinton participating in a scene from season 7; Misha Collins, Hinton, Jensen Ackles and Jared Padalecki; a portrait of Hinton.

relate. The humor! From Dean's smart-ass remarks and shameless flirting to Sam's eye-roll responses to the brothers pranking each other, you can always count on a good dose of humor in a *Supernatural* episode, and I have always believed that laughter is a huge part of living.

In his response Eric told me *The Outsiders* had changed his life and offered to arrange a set visit. Of course, I took him up on that offer.

Fortunately I think that inadvertent squeal was my only embarrassing moment. I managed to shake hands with Jared Padalecki and Jensen Ackles without swooning. I watched Phil Sgriccia direct "Yellow Fever" without getting in the way or knocking over a lamp. Jim Beaver and I talked about Oklahoma and struck up a friendship that has lasted to this day.

The one thing I remember most about that first visit was the kind welcome I received from everyone: the director, the crew, the actors, the caterers. Even though he was in the hospital battling cancer, executive producer Kim Manners sent me a *Supernatural* ball cap from the hospital. I was invited to have my picture taken in the Impala. (It was several years later before I developed the nerve to ask Jared and Jensen for a picture together.)

In all it was a great visit. My only regret? I left the day before Jensen did his now-infamous lip-sync to "Eye of the Tiger," damn it.

Since then I received invitations to return. I've been traveling to the set once or twice a year now for many years, and I am treated like one of the family. I have close friends in all the departments. There's even a director's chair with my name on it.

It's easy to see why people love this kind of work. A new set of problems every day, a new set period often. You could be in Heaven, Hell, Purgatory, Bobby Singer's cabin, the Men of Letters' bunker or a well-designed motel room.

So nowadays, when people ask me what it's like to visit the *Supernatural* set, I say, "It's like going home."

The Road Ahead

WHAT'S WAITING FOR THE WINCHESTERS

ILLUSTRATION BY KAGAN McLEOD

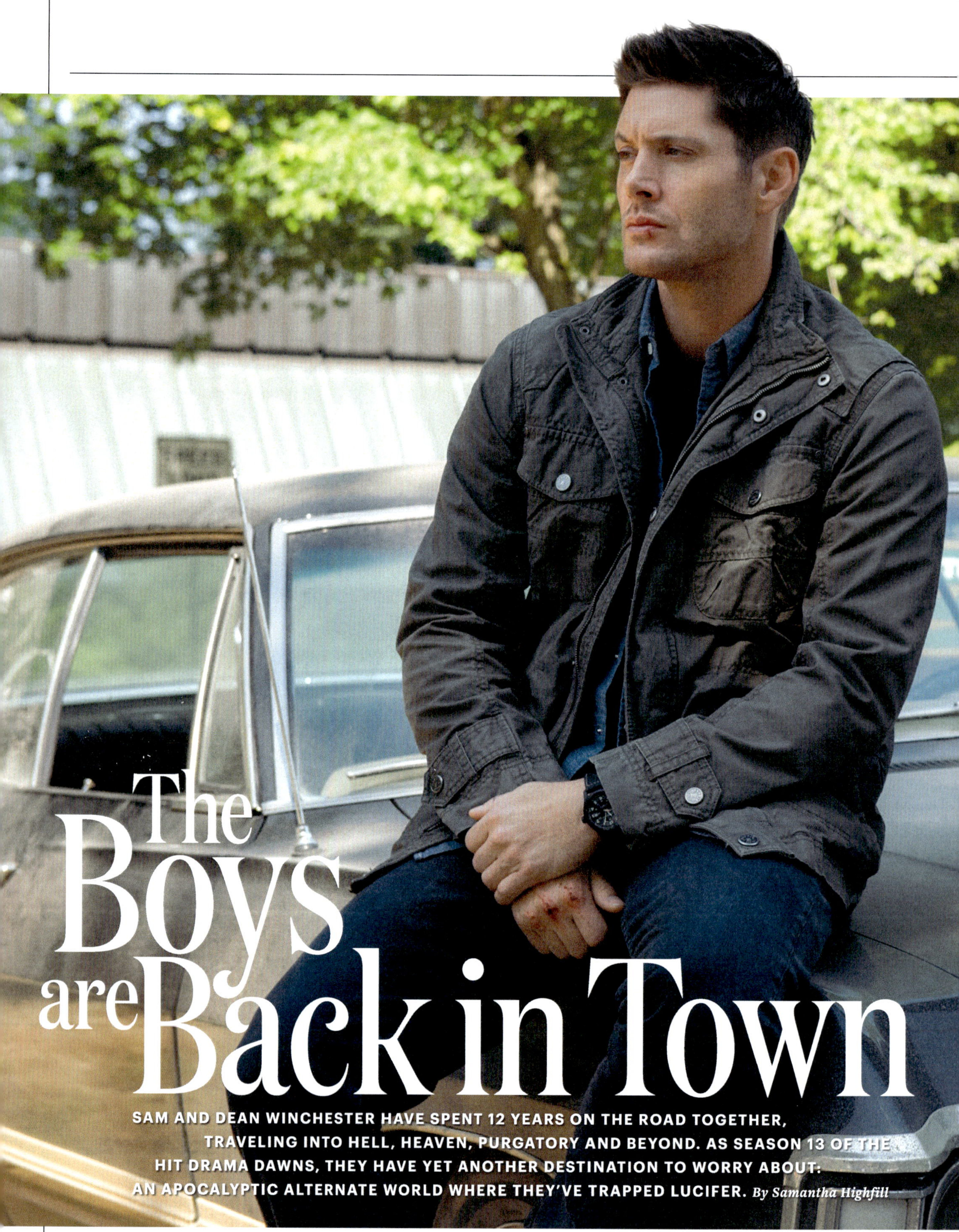

The Boys are Back in Town

SAM AND DEAN WINCHESTER HAVE SPENT 12 YEARS ON THE ROAD TOGETHER, TRAVELING INTO HELL, HEAVEN, PURGATORY AND BEYOND. AS SEASON 13 OF THE HIT DRAMA DAWNS, THEY HAVE YET ANOTHER DESTINATION TO WORRY ABOUT: AN APOCALYPTIC ALTERNATE WORLD WHERE THEY'VE TRAPPED LUCIFER. *By Samantha Highfill*

Dean (Jensen Ackles) and Sam (Jared Padalecki)

SAM AND DEAN WINCHESTER KNOW "WEIRD." Their entire life has been weird, ever since the moment a demon claimed their mother's life. In case anyone has forgotten over the course of the show's past 12 seasons, *Supernatural* tells the story of the Winchester brothers, portrayed by Jared Padalecki and Jensen Ackles, who fell into the family business of hunting creatures after their mother's murder. What began as their father's journey for revenge has evolved into endless monster slayings, near-death experiences and more than a few actual deaths.

By this point the Winchesters have been to Hell and back, killed Death himself, come face-to-face with God and prevented the Apocalypse. But perhaps more impressively, the series has survived three network presidents, five showrunners, a writers' strike and five different time slots. Turns out the only thing harder to kill than the Winchesters is the series itself. "It's one of those shows that has moved a lot, and yet each time it has found that core audience and built on it," Warner Bros. Television president Peter Roth says. "It's been an unsung hero."

If anyone knows about being an unsung hero, it's Sam (Padalecki) and Dean (Ackles), who've dedicated their lives to saving others and asked for nothing in return. Seriously, how many nights have they spent sleeping in their car? And yet that on-the-road lifestyle has paved the way for a number of the show's riskier episodes, which play a crucial role in keeping the audience engaged. In 2015 "Baby" was told entirely from the perspective of their beloved 1967 Impala, and that's not even close to the craziest thing the show's tried.

Aside from the rules the show creates within its canon—yes, they have a historian in the writers' room to keep them honest—not even the sky is the limit when it comes to story ideas. "[Show creator] Eric [Kripke] used to say, 'Smoke 'em if you've got 'em,' which meant: Anything crazy, don't be afraid to run it by us," executive producer Robert Singer says.

That motto led most famously to season 6's "The French Mistake," in which Sam and Dean found themselves in an alternate universe where everyone mistook them for Jared Padalecki and Jensen Ackles, the stars of a show called *Supernatural.* "Our show's not bound by reality," Ackles, 39, says. "We're rooted in reality, but we're not bound by it. That gives us a fifth wall almost."

But *Supernatural*'s season 12 finale managed to raise the stakes by somehow introducing the boys to something they'd never seen before: a world in which they don't exist and Heaven and Hell are locked in an eternal war. By episode's end, their allies Castiel (Misha Collins) and Crowley (Mark Sheppard) were dead, and their mother, Mary (Samantha Smith), who was resurrected—by God's sister!—in the season 11 finale, found herself trapped in this new reality with the Archangel Lucifer (Mark Pellegrino). If that doesn't seem bad enough, the birth of Lucifer's son is the very thing that opened the rift to this

▲
Left: Lucifer's Nephilim son Jack (Alexander Calvert) meets the Winchesters. Right: Scooby-Win!

◀
Sam meets the newborn Jack.

apocalyptic realm. "The world in which Sam and Dean were never born is not a good world," showrunner Andrew Dabb says. "It speaks to the importance of our guys. The world Sam and Dean live in is certainly not perfect, but it's a whole hell of a lot better than the alternative."

Dabb describes the new run of episodes as more melancholy than last year's, with new threats including some long-dead characters. And somehow Scooby-Doo has a role to play. (More on that later.)

"Last season was, in some ways, a very upbeat season for us," says Dabb, who goes on to explain that season 13 will be "darker." In their grief the boys will butt heads when it comes to both Lucifer's son Jack—Dean wants nothing to do with him; Sam thinks he's worth trying to save—and Mary, whom Sam refuses to give up on despite Dean's having lost hope that she's still alive. "The Apocalypse world hangs over our guys a little bit like a sword of Damocles," Dabb says of the season's beginning. "We're definitely going to spend a little time there."

And of course Sam and Dean have this new responsibility thrust upon them before they've had the chance to properly grieve their many losses, including Castiel, who Dabb says will appear, though maybe not the way fans are expecting. "We're not looking to hit the reset button," Dabb says. "We want to give both our guys an opportunity to react to that and ask the question: How would that affect them if their closest friend sacrifices himself for them? There is a certain amount, especially when you look at Dean, of survivor's guilt."

That being said, there will be at least one (animated!) moment of levity, though it's in the season's back half. Episode 16 will be a much-anticipated *Scooby-Doo* crossover, for which Ackles, Padalecki and Collins have already recorded the audio. "They've often talked about *Supernatural* crossing over into something," Ackles says. "I love that it's *Scooby-Doo*."

But even with exciting new ideas on the agenda, there's always the lingering question of how much longer the show can continue. According to CW president Mark Pedowitz, the answer is as long as the guys are happy and the ratings are relatively stable. As for Ackles and Padalecki, they are focusing on the next milestone: hitting 300 episodes (something that would take them 13 episodes into season 14). However, if Sam and Dean have taught the actors anything, it's that Death can be lurking around every corner (and he's usually eating pizza). "If we don't make it to 300, I think Ackles and I will both be truly bummed," Padalecki, 35, says.

Ackles adds, "They're paying us to bring that little bit of magic to what they wrote, and I still feel that magic. The day that I don't feel that magic will be a very sad day, and I hope that day never comes. I'd like to get to 300 before that day comes."

One thing everyone can agree on is that they want to know when the end is nigh. "I think it would be bad for this show to just ride off into the sunset without a finale," Singer says. "I think we've earned that." Ultimately the only thing that's certain about *Supernatural*'s eventual end is the fate of Sam and Dean's Impala, Baby. "He gets Baby," Padalecki says of Ackles. "I get Baby Two." Ackles makes one correction: "No, you'll get Three. Two is a stunt car. It's beat to s---."

But nobody gets Baby just yet. For now they'll need all the Impalas they can get as they try to solve the problems of not one world but two.

Lucifer (Mark Pellegrino) and Mary Winchester (Samantha Smith) survey the war-torn landscape of their new world, littered with corpses

Left to right: Keep a guardian angel on your night table with this FUNKO DORBZ mini Castiel; a 1:64 scale Impala ready for the road; the cover and illustrated page from *The Men of Letters Bestiary*, one of many tie-in titles now available.

YOU AIN'T SEEN NOTHING YET

In these candid on-set shots, we catch glimpses of the affable ensemble goofing off, pranking one another and even taking turns directing episodes. **BY SAMANTHA HIGHFILL**

▲ While it's not unusual for Collins to be holding an angel blade, why, in this photo taken during season 8, is he aiming it at Dean? Better question: Why is there a sketch of Dean in the props room?

▶ In 2006 Jensen Ackles takes a break to check out a shot while filming season 2's "Playthings," in which Sam and Dean deal with a ghost. Eagle-eyed fans will notice something else about this photo: Dean's wearing the amulet that Sam gave him when they were kids (and that will later be used to identify Chuck as God).

▲ Fans know Richard Speight Jr. best for his role as Gabriel, the Trickster revealed as Archangel who was killed by Lucifer in season 5. In season 11 Speight directed his first episode, "Just My Imagination," which investigated a serial killer targeting imaginary friends. (Yes, that is a mermaid in the grave.)

◀ Executive producer and director Kim Manners—seen here talking with Jared Padalecki and Genevieve Padalecki (née Cortese), who played Ruby in season 4—was a beloved member of the *Supernatural* family. Manners died in the middle of season 4 after battling cancer. The last episode he directed was "Metamorphosis."

▲
Castiel's wearing a T-shirt?! Not so much. Actor Misha Collins directed season 9's "Mother's Little Helper," which took place at the start of the Mark of Cain story line (and wasn't nearly as upbeat as this photo).

▶
The first time Ackles stepped behind the camera to direct was season 6's "Weekend at Bobby's." So by the time "The Bad Seed" rolled around in season 11, the by-then five-time director was feeling fully confident. Here he chats with the King of Hell, Mark Sheppard. Far right: For Padalecki and Ackles (seen here between shots for season 8), the off-camera brotherhood was firmly cemented quite quickly. "There was an instant connection," says Ackles, recalling that he knew their dynamic was going to work from the first time they met and read together. "We had a lot of things in common right off the bat."

Razor
SUSIES SALOON
AMSTERDAM
O.Z. VOORBURGWAL 254

LIFE IN THE FAST LANE

EXCLUSIVE INTERVIEW

Stars Jensen Ackles, Jared Padalecki and Misha Collins have rolled with rapid changes and some surprising detours during the series' remarkable run. **BY SAMANTHA HIGHFILL**

JARED PADALECKI CAN STILL REMEMBER THE exact pitch for *Supernatural*'s first season: "*Route 66* meets *X-Files*, brothers on the back roads of America hunting things that go bump in the night." That was how he and costar Jensen Ackles were told to promote the show, which, in its first year, was just that—Sam and Dean Winchester chasing urban legends from state to state.

But over time that original pitch added a few sentences. Much like with any good road trip, there have been quite a few turns—and the occasional crossroads—along the way. Although the show remains about two brothers on the back roads of America hunting things, those "things" now include everything from vengeful spirits to imaginary friends and even Lucifer himself. After all, a show doesn't last 13 seasons without adjusting its game plan. For *Supernatural* that has meant an ever-expanding mythology, some shocking deaths, resurrected characters, breaking the fourth wall and so much more.

Yet all the while, one thing has remained true: Sam and Dean Winchester will do whatever it takes to save the world and, even more so, to save each other. And they'll do it while navigating those seemingly endless back roads in their 1967 Impala.

Jensen Ackles, Jared Padalecki and Misha Collins goof off at *EW*'s photo booth in 2017.

PHOTOGRAPHS BY MATTHIAS CLAMER

"We didn't want to be a mouthpiece for writers' religious views, because it wasn't the show that we had signed up for"
–Jensen Ackles

Finding John Winchester (portrayed by Jeffrey Dean Morgan) was the boys' goal in season 1, though that ended up being about as difficult as getting John to stick around once he was finally discovered. The Winchester family reunion was short-lived: Season 1 closed with a car crash and the fates of all three men up in the air. And then there was that demonic deal John made with the same monster they had been hunting.

JENSEN ACKLES Everything up until that point was about finding Dad. We found Dad, we continued to fight as a unit, and then we lost Dad, and now we were two orphans.

JARED PADALECKI And I think that was the first time we ever brought back somebody from the dead, and it was you [*to Ackles*].

ACKLES I died in the car crash, and he traded his life with Azazel.

PADALECKI I think that was the first time we ever saw a major character die and come back. And that was a total leap of faith. So we told the story of Reapers and the veil and what happens to your soul.

ACKLES That's when we got into afterlife.

PADALECKI That was a big title shift in what *Supernatural* could do...

ACKLES With the introduction of Hell and making deals with demons—which is funny, because you think about that now, and [creator] Eric [Kripke] must've always known because Mom made the deal with the yellow-eyed demon.

The next shift would come later in season 2, laying the groundwork for the introduction of angels far before Castiel spread his wings in that abandoned barn in season 4.

PADALECKI "Houses of the Holy" was the first time we ever talked about angels on *Supernatural*. [Jensen] and I both were like, "Whatever your religious beliefs, whatever ours, we're not here to proselytize. We're here to make a serialized television show, but we want it to be universal." So we actually had a conference call with Eric Kripke, and we were like, "Hey, man, we don't know how we feel about this."

ACKLES We didn't want to be a mouthpiece for writers' religious views, because it wasn't the show that we had signed up for. Our argument was: "We trust you. You've done good by us so far. However, this is our one concern, and we're just bringing it to the table so that we can discuss it."

PADALECKI And they heard us out, and I think that's why they waited another year

and a half before introducing our second and most famous angel. I think it's the one time we've ever called them together with a complaint. Because I'm not a writer. I don't want to be a writer. I enjoy my job as an actor. But that was legitimately like, "Listen, if you're going here about religion, I don't want to be a part of it."

MISHA COLLINS And now amazingly, 11 years later, so much of the show has been hung on biblical lore and mythology that is actually drawn from the Bible. One interesting thing for us is that we end up talking along the way to priests and pastors and ministers, or even nuns, who love the show.

ACKLES [*To Collins*] You and I went to the Vatican. We went in St. Peter's Basilica, and there was a priest there from South Carolina. He was a fan of the show, and he did a private mass for us in front of the mural of Michael slaying Lucifer. He goes, "I thought this would be appropriate for you guys."

COLLINS That was pretty magical.

ACKLES It was amazing, but my point being that we're in one of the most religious places on earth, and they're catering to people from a show that deals with religiously inspired story lines.

PADALECKI But not telling the story that the Bible tells.

ACKLES That's the out. That's where we get a pass is that we're not trying to tell the story of the Bible. The writers take inspiration from biblical elements and then elaborate on them. So when we got into that original discussion, Eric came back with: "We're not here to tell the story of Jesus Christ. We're here to take that element and use it as inspiration for the story." I think that alleviated any concerns that he and I had. And at the same time we really trusted Eric and still do to this day.

Another leap of faith came with season 2's "Hollywood Babylon," which can be considered the show's first meta episode. It opened the door for everything from season 6's "The French Mistake" to the upcoming season 13 Scooby-Doo *crossover.*

ACKLES "Babylon" was the first time we took the piss out of ourselves and were poking fun at the industry.

COLLINS That has been a huge [help to know] that you can go to these absurd lengths and break conventions. Reading the script where we are doing a *Scooby-Doo* episode makes me feel proud. Where else can you do that?

PADALECKI What other show does that *and* has the fandom at large excited that they're going to do that? Can you imagine if *JAG* or *NCIS* did a *Scooby-Doo* episode? People would be like, "What?" Not only do we break the fourth wall, do we go meta, but those end up being some of our best episodes.

The season 5 finale holds the No. 1 spot on EW*'s episode ranking, but that hour was important for many reasons, one of which being that it was creator Kripke's farewell.*

COLLINS "Swan Song" was another milestone because that marked the culmination of Eric's original vision for the show. He had a five-season arc in mind that tied up perfectly with a bow, and then he moved on and handed the reins over to Sera [Gamble]. That became, "Okay, guys, now let's figure out how to start a new chapter or a new volume in a series of chapters."

PADALECKI It's the story that we were all born from, those of us who were introduced in the first five years. So to have the creator step away? I would argue that it was the largest shift.

Gamble served as showrunner for seasons 6 and 7, the latter containing another major show moment: the death of Bobby (Jim Beaver), Sam and Dean's father figure.

PADALECKI Bobby was such a big part. Jeffrey Dean [Morgan] was never as much a part of the show. He was obviously a huge part of the story, but he did [just a few] episodes, and Jim Beaver did 60 or something. And there was something about his death that we knew it was final…or final for *Supernatural.*

ACKLES Because his character said, "I'm done." So it wasn't like he got killed accidentally and we found a way to bring Bobby back. He was like, "I'm hanging it up, guys." It was heavy.

PADALECKI That probably was the first big death of someone who'd been there for years…

ACKLES [*Interrupting*] A fan favorite…

PADALECKI Yeah, and I remember [CW

president] Mark Pedowitz saying something to the effect of "As a fan, I hated when Bobby died, but it was great television." That's how I feel.

ACKLES Like when Sam Winchester dies for good, it's going to be good television. But when Dean Winchester lives on, it's going to be great television. [*Everyone laughs*]

The season 12 finale saw the introduction of an apocalyptic alternate world in which Sam and Dean Winchester were never born and Heaven and Hell are locked in an eternal war. And with that world comes the possibility for a number of character returns. But does it feel like a turning point?

COLLINS Well, I think the rift and the fact that you can go into the apocalypse world and you can all of a sudden revisit every character in a different iteration—there could be a different version of every character—it opens up this incredible panoply.

ACKLES Why not have the same characters as something different?

PADALECKI And if an alternate universe exists, then how many alternate universes exist? It's hard to say, because I feel like it's impossible to identify a turning point during the turn. In hindsight it will reveal how this story will affect the show, the canon at large and the way we move forward. But I certainly feel like we're opening up doors with the rift and with the son of Lucifer.

COLLINS It's also hard because [in] the first five years there were all of these totally mind-blowing new chapters that were opened. So much stuff has been taken to such extremes that it's hard to go to a new extreme that's so big that it blows that whole world open again.

PADALECKI It's almost like a paradox, but we tell these stories in a way that's based in reality. This is not a fantastical show. This isn't a long time ago in a galaxy far, far away. Part of our whole premise is that this is this world. We're telling crazy stories, but this is in the world you live in right now. It's neat to see our writers, who are incredibly talented, weave that in and try to fit a square peg in a round hole. It's neat to watch and be a part of.

Angels & Demons

ILLUSTRATION BY KAGAN McLEOD

Seeking to put a murderous spirit to rest, Dean salts and burns the bones of a man who murdered 13 women in the 19th century with his silver-hook prosthesis.

They're on the Highway to Hell

_EW_ TAKES A ROAD TRIP TO VANCOUVER TO BREAK BREAD WITH _SUPERNATURAL'S_ HEARTTHROB STARS AND TO TAKE THE PULSE OF ITS SPOOKY, KOOKY AND ALTOGETHER EXTRAORDINARY RUN.

By Samantha Highfill

T

THE CORONER'S VAN JUST PULLED INTO THE driveway. It's the middle of August in 2016, and Jared Padalecki and Jensen Ackles are filming a scene for *Supernatural*'s 12th season at a farmhouse in the Vancouver countryside, which is standing in for Iowa. Sam and Dean Winchester have ditched their flannels and jeans for sweaters and slacks in order to pose as social workers. They're doing what the two brothers do best: lying about their jobs in order to solve mysteries and kill monsters—in other words, saving people, hunting things.

When *Supernatural* premiered, Sam and Dean Winchester were born into the family business of hunting creatures, and it's a lifestyle that, over the years, has left them with very few people they love. Turns out, when you spend your days battling shape-shifters, witches and the occasional angel—they're not all nice, you know—nothing is guaranteed, especially not tomorrow.

But no matter how crazy the Winchesters' world gets—or how many worlds they have to face—one thing remains unchanged: At the center of it all are Ackles and Padalecki, whose Dean and Sam are the beating heart of the show (whether theirs are beating or not).

As they sit down to dinner in Vancouver, the brotherhood between the two—who both live in Austin when they're not filming—is on full display as they finish each other's sentences and argue about how Padalecki ate the last piece of tuna. "The familiarity was there pretty quickly, which I think is which is why we got the job," Ackles says of the day he and Padalecki

▲

Above left: At Harvelle's Roadhouse, former MIT student Ash (Chad Lindberg) helps research while Jo (Alona Tal) looks on. Above right: An emotional reunion between father and sons. Below: Castiel (Misha Collins) considers the implication of a broken Devil's Trap.

◀

Far left: Bobby Singer (Jim Beaver) fights off the spirits of twin girls who were killed by a monster he failed to find. Left: Dean and Bela (Lauren Cohan) go undercover.

auditioned for the studio. "There was an instant connection. We had a lot of things in common right off the bat. Then they came out and said, 'Congratulations guys, you got the job,' and I thought, 'Okay I could certainly work with this guy for as long as they let us.'" (Spoiler alert: With the show heading into its 13th season, that has ended up being a very long time.)

And yet, that chemistry has only grown stronger over the years. In fact, the stars are still eager to talk about why they love their show, even pulling up their favorite scenes on their phones to watch at the table. Padalecki can easily name the scripts that made him cry—"Heart," "Sacrifice" and "Baby" all land on the list. The common thread is a heartfelt moment between the brothers where they get to talk about their crazy life as if, say, having visions of Lucifer is normal. "I feel like those situations where we treat the abstract and the fantastical as just part of life is where the show thrives," Padalecki says. Ackles adds, "I think the show is truly at its best when it doesn't take itself too seriously, then it does take itself seriously, and it gets scary as s---."

But whether *Supernatural* is making fun of itself, scaring the living daylights out of its fans, or just letting the brothers have a moment on the hood of the Impala, it all works because of our central heroes. "It's about the Winchesters," says Crowley actor Mark Sheppard. "We really do care, and it's a testament to the boys that we still care."

Ackles adds, "We've been doing this consistently for a long, long time. There is a silent language that he and I have." That silent language also works at dinner, as when Ackles gives Padalecki a look when he reaches across the table and steals some steak sauce. "I can pass it to you," Ackles says as Padalecki laughs.

As the sun sets on the Vancouver countryside, Sam and Dean ditch their slacks for jeans and send the coroner's van on its way. It won't be needed—this show, and the brotherly bond that holds it all together, has a lot of life left in it. Not that death has ever stopped it before.

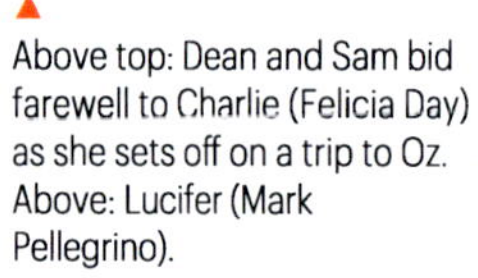

▲ Above top: Dean and Sam bid farewell to Charlie (Felicia Day) as she sets off on a trip to Oz. Above: Lucifer (Mark Pellegrino).

► Cain (Timothy Omundson) reunites with the First Blade.

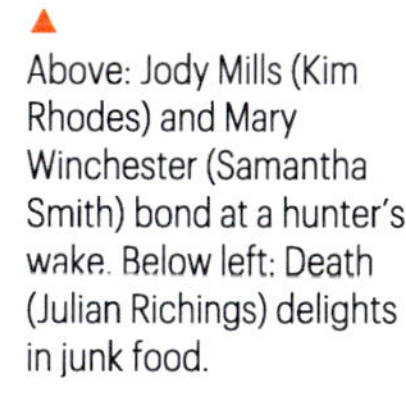

Above: Jody Mills (Kim Rhodes) and Mary Winchester (Samantha Smith) bond at a hunter's wake. Below left: Death (Julian Richings) delights in junk food.

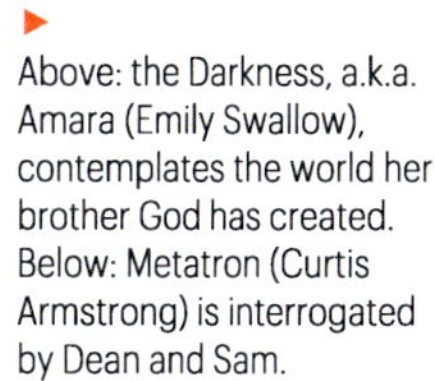

Above: the Darkness, a.k.a. Amara (Emily Swallow), contemplates the world her brother God has created. Below: Metatron (Curtis Armstrong) is interrogated by Dean and Sam.

Born to Be Wild

THE BROTHERS WOULD GO TO HELL FOR EACH OTHER, AND HAVE. BUT THE WINCHESTER CLAN EXTENDS BEYOND DEAN AND SAM—MEET THE MEMBERS OF THE WORLD'S MOST DEADLY FAMILY BUSINESS. *By Alyssa Smith*

Sam (Jared Padalecki), left, and Dean Winchester (Jensen Ackles)

SAM WINCHESTER
Jared Padalecki

The younger, more rebellious Winchester brother, Sam had no interest in paranormal activity—rather, he dreamed of law school and set off for Stanford with no plans ever to return home. That decision led to a years-long estrangement from his brother Dean and his father, John. Things changed, though, when one day Dean dropped by asking for help ("Dad's on a hunting trip. And he hasn't been home in a few days"). Sam came to his brother's aid—and sadly soon had his own reason to rejoin the hunt: After his girlfriend suffered the same fiery death as his mom, he vowed revenge against Yellow Eyes, also known as the demon Azazel. Since resuming the hunter's life, Sam has died around a half dozen times (none of them stuck). He's visited both Heaven and Hell (to return Lucifer to his Cage), been possessed by demons and angels, and generally saved the world—a lot.

DEAN WINCHESTER
Jensen Ackles

He was always the good son. Dean embraced the hunter's lifestyle, and he idolized his father despite John's many faults. But with the senior Winchester devoted to tracking down demons, it fell to Dean to help parent Sam, and he went to great lengths to protect his younger sibling—at one point even making a deal with a Crossroads demon (at the cost of his own life) to resurrect Sam from the dead. The two have had their differences, but throughout, Dean's brother was his first priority. "Watching out for you, it's kinda been my job, you know? But more than that, it's kinda who I am." Cynical and initially skeptical of the existence of God, Dean has nonetheless managed to become best buds with the angel Castiel (and on first-name terms with both God and God's sister Amara). His self-sacrificing nature means he would do literally anything for those he considers family—and that's a short list: Sam, Mary and Castiel.

MARY WINCHESTER
Samantha Smith; Amy Gumenick

Born into a family of hunters, Mary Winchester (née Campbell) only wanted a normal life for her children. But her dream never came true. A deal with Yellow Eyes to bring John back from the dead had terrible repercussions for the Winchesters, Mary most of all.

JOHN WINCHESTER
Jeffrey Dean Morgan; Matt Cohen

The mysterious death of his wife turned the former Marine into a vengeance-mad hunter. Obsessed with finding Azazel and making him pay for Mary's death, John raised his two small boys on the road, teaching them about monsters as they traveled from town to town.

ADAM MILLIGAN
Jake Abel

By the time Sam and Dean learned they had a younger half brother, Adam was already dead—though that didn't stop Archangel Michael from using Adam as his vessel during the Apocalypse. When that went south, both Adam and Michael ended up in Lucifer's Cage.

TOOLS OF THE TRADE

When only the right weapon will finish the job, it takes an ever-expanding arsenal to slay mythical monsters. Fortunately the boys have plenty at their disposal. **BY ALYSSA SMITH**

THE WORD OF GOD

Narrated to Metatron by God himself, the Word of God tablets contain priceless information on how to control, contain and defeat demons, angels and Leviathan. Unfortunately they can only be read by a Prophet of the Lord.

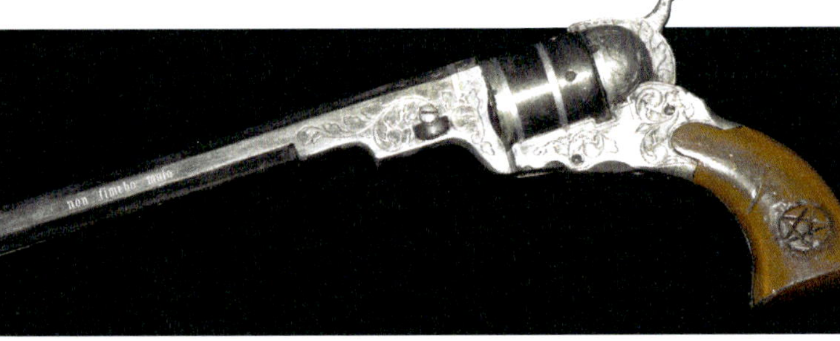

THE COLT

The legendary revolver, built by Samuel Colt himself in 1835, frequently has been in the possession of the Winchesters. According to old hunters' tales, there are only five beings in creation who cannot be slain by its 13 original bullets. (Thankfully, when those were used up, Bobby Singer managed to jury-rig more ammo.)

DEVIL'S TRAP

As discussed in the book *Key of Solomon*, this multisided star within a circle can contain a demon, rendering it powerless. The five-sided version can be created using a simple can of spray paint.

1

HOLY WATER

It's a classic: Just a splash of holy water will burn a demon, allowing hunters to quickly identify a possessed meatsuit.

2

WOODEN STAKE

Simple but often effective, a wooden stake can paralyze a demon, kill a deity and dispatch some kinds of zombies.

3

RUBY'S KNIFE

The rare item that can slay rank-and-file demons, this ancient knife was given to the Winchesters by the demon Ruby. (They later killed her with it.)

4

SILVER KNIFE

Many monsters descended from Eve either find silver intolerable or are slain by a silver knife to the heart.

5

SILVER BULLETS

Guns retrofitted to use silver ammo are effective against a variety of enemies, including werewolves, skinwalkers and shape-shifters.

Meet Baby

PAINT IT BLACK

God called the brothers' Impala "the most important object in pretty much the whole universe." It has been totaled, rebuilt and totaled again. But for the Winchesters, one thing remains constant: It's home sweet home. **BY ALYSSA SMITH**

Sam and Dean case out a potential job from the safety of their beloved muscle car.

Chevrolet
CNK 80Q3

SPECIAL FEATURES

Dean and Sam's weapons arsenal, concealed beneath a false floor in the trunk, is just one of the unique details of their '67 Impala. (Originally shown with Kansas plates, it suddenly bears Ohio tags starting in season 2.) As kids, while living out of the vehicle with their father, the two brothers carved their initials in the floor, jammed a plastic Army-man figure into the ashtray and shoved Lego down the air-conditioner vents.

ORIGIN STORY

In an alternate world, the family car might have been a VW van. Fortunately a time-traveling Dean, using the alias Van Halen, offered some helpful advice to a young John Winchester at a used-car lot in 1973. When Dean comes of age, his father gives him the car.

BEHIND THE SCENES

Numerous Impalas have been used during filming. The mint vehicle seen in nearly every episode is nicknamed Baby One. Car coordinator Jeff Budnick manages a warehouse full of Impala parts to keep the show's fleet rolling. Once the show ends, two cars are already spoken for: Baby One will go home with Ackles, and Padalecki will drive away with Baby Three. (Two is a stunt automobile.)

▷ SAM & DEAN'S PLAYLIST

Carry On Wayward Son Kansas

Back in Black AC/DC

Eye of the Tiger Survivor

Rock of Ages Def Leppard

A Well Respected Man The Kinks

Heat of the Moment Asia

Wanted Dead or Alive Bon Jovi

Back on the Road Again REO Speedwagon

Thunderstruck AC/DC

Superstition Beck Bogert & Appice

PEOPLE ARE STRANGE

More than a few famous faces have turned up over the course of *Supernatural*'s 12 seasons, often as the monster of the week, sometimes as a terrified victim, more rarely as a new ally to the Winchesters. **BY ALYSSA SMITH**

1

DEE WALLACE
Mildred Baker

Scream queen Wallace (*The Stepford Wives, Cujo, E.T.*) played the worldly-wise Mildred, who was savvy enough to see right through the Winchesters' cover ("You two are too cute to be FBI agents"). She helped them defeat the banshee haunting her home.

2

RICK SPRINGFIELD
Vince Vincente/Lucifer

Lucifer entered another vessel in season 12: musician and actor Rick Springfield ("Jessie's Girl"). Springfield rocked a guitar in his multi-episode arc, parodying himself as a washed-up star reuniting his band Ladyheart. (That's when we learned Dean is not a fan of '80s hair metal.)

UNION

3
4
5
6
7-8

9

10

11

3

GARY COLE
Brad Redding

The *Office Space* and *Veep* star shows up on a movie set as the boys look into a murder. The hotshot studio executive is short-lived (death by ghost). But at least one element of the character was grounded in truth: Every note he gives the film's director is something the CW told the *Supernatural* makers at some point. (Why *are* ghosts afraid of salt?)

4

BARRY BOSTWICK
Jay

Bostwick (*Spin City, The Rocky Horror Picture Show*) stars as a has-been magician who suddenly gets his groove back in the season 4 episode "Criss Angel Is a Douchebag."

5

JULIE BENZ
Layla Rourke

Benz was the first *Buffy* veteran to appear on *Supernatural.* The memorable season 1 episode "Faith" also introduced the monstrous Reapers—and included a pitch-perfect moment featuring Blue Öyster Cult's "(Don't Fear) the Reaper."

6

PARIS HILTON
Leshii

It's been a while since 2005's *House of Wax,* but when Hilton reunites with her former costar Padalecki, it's worth the wait. She's a Leshii, a shape-shifting god that takes on the form of any object of worship.

7-8

JAMES MARSTERS & CHARISMA CARPENTER
Don and Maggie Stark

Buffy alums Marsters and Carpenter share the screen as a married (but feuding) pair of witches. Naturally the boys get stuck in the middle.

9

LINDA BLAIR
Detective Diana Ballard

Sam and Dean are rounded up as suspects in a homicide investigation, but the detective on the case, film legend Blair (*The Exorcist*), begins to think they aren't actually the killers. When she's proven right—and the Winchesters save her life—she lets them go. "Did she look familiar to you?" asks Dean. "For some reason I could really go for some pea soup."

10

MERCEDES McNAB
Lucy

Poor, doomed Lucy. McNab (yet another *Buffy* actor) riffs on her former role on Joss Whedon's series, playing a woman who has been unknowingly turned into a vampire.

11

NICOLE 'SNOOKI' POLIZZI
Demon

"What's a Snooki?" asks Sam in season 6. The MTV reality star nonchalantly appears after the boys summon a crossroads demon. Actually, she says, "it's Nicole now."

Mark Pellegrino joined the show in season 5 as Lucifer. Although the role would be played by many actors over the years, Pellegrino has proved to be Lucifer's most consistent vessel.

Sympathy for the Devil

EVERY HERO NEEDS A HEEL, BUT *SUPERNATURAL* HAS JUST TWO PROTAGONISTS AND HUNDREDS OF VILLAINS. HERE'S HOW THE SHOWRUNNERS APPROACHED SAM AND DEAN'S MANY FOES, FROM WELL-KNOWN URBAN LEGENDS TO SATAN HIMSELF.

By Samantha Highfill

I

IT ALL STARTED WITH A DEMON. THE Yellow-Eyed Demon, to be exact. Before Sam and Dean were old enough to understand what was happening, Azazel killed their mother and unknowingly sealed their fate. With their father hell-bent on revenge, Sam and Dean were thrust into a world filled with vampires, vengeful spirits, werewolves and even bugs (though, thankfully, only that one time).

In its early days *Supernatural* focused much more heavily on the so-called monsters of the week. Sam and Dean weren't spending seasons trying to stop the Apocalypse; rather, they were spending days trying to stop, say, a wendigo. Week after week they would hunt the likes of Hook Man, Bloody Mary and just about any baddies from the stories you'd hear around a bonfire at summer camp. "[Show creator] Eric [Kripke] was very specific about what he thought the show should be," says executive producer Robert Singer. "Eric originally would say, 'You have to have Google-able monsters or Google-able urban legends.'" But when it became apparent that the show would eventually run out of existing urban legends, it began building longer mythologies in addition to the monsters of the week.

Yet no matter how long they stuck around, there was one thing all monsters had in common: a narrative. "We try to give them their own personality," Singer says of the show's villains. "They're not cardboard-cutout monsters. I don't know how many vampires we've done over the years, but they each have their own story."

In season 5 the show took that idea and applied it specifically to two of the longest-running villains. First up, Sam accidentally freed Lucifer from the Cage, thereby introducing the Winchesters'—and the world's—biggest foe. "I directed the first episode that Mark Pellegrino was in, and right away you could see this was not somebody we wanted to lose," Singer says of the show's most frequent portrayer of Lucifer.

And the same went for another season 5 addition: "When we saw [Mark Sheppard] as [Crowley] the King of the Crossroads, we said, 'God, this guy's terrific. He's a great character to write for. How do we put him into the main fabric of the show?'" Singer recalls thinking. "We like to do that. When characters just seem to jump off the screen, we're always finding ways to bring them back [for more episodes]."

Not only did Crowley come back, but he got a promotion. When Sam and Dean successfully trapped Lucifer in the Cage again at the end of season 5 (where he'd remain until season 11) Crowley suddenly became the new King of Hell, and therefore a central villain—and sometimes friend—of the Winchesters'. And as the seasons went on, that friendship only grew. "He's actually been more benevolent than malevolent throughout the years," Sheppard says of his character.

Nothing proved that more than Crowley's demise in the season 12 finale, when he sacrificed himself to help the Winchesters trap Lucifer. After all, nobody can take out the King of Hell like the King of Hell.

▲ Left: Ruby, mark one, played by Katie Cassidy. She returns in a different meatsuit in season 4. Right: Sam interrogates a captured Crowley (Mark Sheppard).

◀ Left: The demon Alastair (Christopher Heyerdahl), known as Hell's Grand Torturer, meets his end. Right: Borax is especially harmful to Leviathan, which is why we see Meg (Rachel Miner) using it to her advantage.

WHO'S WHO... IN HELL

Regardless of the color of their eyes, the demonic horde created by Lucifer faced the Winchesters as implacable adversaries—and, more rarely, allies. **BY ALYSSA SMITH**

1

2

3

5

6

7

1

MEG MASTERS 1
Nicki Aycox

"Meg" was the name of the black-eyed demon's first human host—and it liked the appellation enough to keep it; unfortunately possession most often leads to death for a human host. During the Rising of the Witnesses, Meg's ghost returned to haunt Dean.

MEG MASTERS 2
Rachel Miner

After Lucifer was re-Caged, Meg, determined to take revenge on Crowley for his role in her master's undoing, found a new host. Still, things didn't end well for her—even with help from the Winchesters.

LUCIFER
Mark Pellegrino

Angels cannot possess a vessel unless the vessel allows it, which complicates things for Lucifer, considering his true vessel is Sam Winchester. The Archangel has body-hopped through beings from the POTUS to Castiel, but his most recent war with the temporary King of Hell led to him reclaim his original vessel, perhaps permanently (thanks for that, Crowley).

CROWLEY
Mark Sheppard

The King of the Crossroads turned King of Hell, Crowley was always ready to cut a deal. In fact, during his first meeting with the Winchesters he sold out Lucifer. Sometimes an ally, more often an antagonist, his final sacrifice in the season 12 finale might have accomplished what God could not: seal Lucifer from Earth.

5

ALASTAIR
Mark Rolston

Hell's "Picasso with a razor," the white-eyed demon wielded power roughly equivalent to Lilith and was more than a match for an angel or two. He body-hopped before being captured by Castiel and meeting his end.

LILITH
Katherine Boecher

In Lucifer's absence, Lilith ruled Hell and led the demonic hosts to break the 66 Seals to release her creator from his Cage. (The final seal? Her death.) The Winchesters weren't torn up: They held a long-standing grudge against the white-eyed demon as it was her hellhound that savaged Dean and sent him to Hell.

CAIN
Timothy Omundson

The Father of Murder and Knight of Hell was once human and a direct ancestor to the Winchesters. His complicated relationship with Dean, to whom he bequeathed the Mark of Cain, eventually led to his death.

8

RUBY 1
Katie Cassidy

First introducing herself to Bobby, Ruby helped the Winchesters to prove her worth almost immediately by fixing the Colt and lending them her exorcism knife.

RUBY 2
Genevieve Cortese

A brain-dead Jane Doe served as the second host for the Lucifer-loyalist and double-agent. Although Sam insisted she harm no more humans, Ruby continued to manipulate him to break seals to free her master.

Stairway to Heaven

SAM AND DEAN MET CASTIEL, AN ANGEL OF THE LORD, IN SEASON 4, AND IT CHANGED THE COURSE OF THE SHOW. BECAUSE ANGELS WEREN'T ALWAYS THE PLAN—AND CASTIEL WAS ONLY THE FIRST.

By Samantha Highfill

In what executive producer Robert Singer calls one of the series' most "iconic images," Castiel (Misha Collins) is introduced as the show's first real angel.

WHILE OTHER CHILDREN WERE LEARNING multiplication tables, Sam and Dean Winchester were hunting monsters. "When I told Dad I was scared of the thing in my closet, he gave me a .45!" says Sam to Dean in the *Supernatural* pilot, recalling an episode when he was 9 years old. Clearly creature encounters were par for the course in the Winchester way of life. And when you grow up battling all the evil in the world, it's hard to believe in the good. But in the show's season 4 premiere, Dean would come face-to-face with the one supernatural entity he didn't think existed: angels.

"[Show creator] Eric [Kripke] wasn't in love with the idea of doing angels," executive producer Robert Singer says of the early days. "But as things went on and we were getting into demons, I would say to him, 'I don't know how we do demons without doing angels.'"

The show tested the waters in season 2's "Houses of the Holy," when Sam and Dean worked a case that appeared to involve angels then went in a different direction. It wasn't until late in the next season that the seraphim were finally embraced. When Dean was dragged to Hell, they needed to get him out. And if there's a Hell, it stands to reason there has to be a Heaven. "[The season 3 finale] was the gateway into this whole other world of angels and demons," executive producer Andrew Dabb says.

When it came time to spring Dean from Hell, it was Castiel, the show's first angel, who gripped him tight and raised him from perdition. But Castiel quickly established that he wasn't a typical cherubic angel. Many of the show's angels were, as Sam and Dean would put it, real dicks. "We have our own brand of angels and the idea that they were these warriors of God," Singer says. "We introduced Castiel, and we just went from there. Heaven opened up different levels of angels."

The moment Castiel spread his wings, the show expanded its universe. Castiel came bearing news of something much bigger: the Apocalypse, the ultimate showdown between good and evil—or more specifically between Archangels Michael and Lucifer. "We started with archangels and the idea that Lucifer was an archangel and was cast out of Heaven," Singer says. "We certainly took some license, but it was all biblically grounded. We just took those things and went a step further to make them work for our story."

From there the show explored all kinds of angels, from Zachariah and Naomi to Gabriel and Metatron, and, of course, it eventually arrived at God—or Chuck, if you prefer. "We didn't really know that Chuck was God when we first started with him," Singer says of introducing the character in season 4. (He wouldn't be revealed as God until season 11.) "That evolved. We wanted a relatable God, a God with foibles."

Nine seasons later, what started as one angel in a trench coat has evolved into Lucifer, God, Leviathan and even a sister for God. "We play a little fast and loose with religion, but no one has really complained about it," Singer says with a laugh. "So we'll just keep going."

Moments after his famous "Hey, ass-butt" line, Castiel torches Michael (Jake Abel) to prevent the Apocalypse.

Left: The Prophet Kevin Tran (Osric Chau) translates one of the tablets containing the Word of God. Right: God himself (Rob Benedict) after asking his scribe (Metatron, far right, played by Curtis Armstrong) to review his memoirs.

WHO'S WHO... IN HEAVEN

As Castiel informed Dean when they first met, the warriors of God are soldiers—and sometimes that means they're at war with the Winchesters. (Looking for Lucifer? We placed him in Hell. His fellow angels would agree it's where he belongs.) **BY ALYSSA SMITH**

1

2

3

5

6

7

1

MICHAEL
Matt Cohen

The oldest of the four archangels, Michael played the role of the good son—a part echoed by the actions of Dean, who was intended to be Michael's true vessel during the apocalyptic showdown with Lucifer.

2

GABRIEL
Richard Speight Jr.

When the Winchesters first met the youngest Archangel, he appeared to be a minor obstacle to defeat: the Trickster. (He's later discovered masquerading as Loki from the Norse pantheon.) *Supernatural*'s masterful reveal of his true identity helped make the multiseason storyline feel seamless.

3

CHUCK/GOD
Rob Benedict

After almost 12 seasons, the awkward writer, introduced as a prophet working on what Castiel referred to as "the Winchester gospels," was actually revealed as the Big Man himself. Having Dean and Sam Winchester exist as characters within their own story has led to some memorable moments (and an even more memorable musical).

4

RAPHAEL
Lanette Ware

After his fellow archangels were killed or imprisoned, Raphael chose to start a war for control of Heaven with Castiel, who betrayed his orders in support of Team Free Will. That doesn't work out well for Raphael, who gets splattered when Castiel absorbs all the souls (and thus the power) in Purgatory.

5

METATRON
Curtis Armstrong

God's scribe described himself as just a "run-of-the-mill" angel before he was selected to write down the Word of God on the tablets. Later he used the knowledge gained from his transcription duties to wage a war for control of Heaven.

6

NAOMI
Amanda Tapping

The death or absence of the archangels left a power vacuum filled by Naomi. Specializing in gathering information from rebellious angels, she controls (and erases) Castiel's mind several times before being slain by Metatron.

7

ZACHARIAH
Kurt Fuller

The powerful angel informed Dean that in his real form, he has "six wings and four faces, one of which is a lion." None of those faces turns out to be much help when Dean stabs him in the jaw with an angel blade.

8

GADREEL
Tahmoh Penikett

Gadreel's failure at the gates of the Garden of Eden allowed Lucifer to corrupt humanity and create demons—which is why when he escaped, he went on the run. Eventually he became Metatron's servant, and his final sacrifice ended Heaven's war.

9

CASTIEL
Misha Collins

What can you say about the only member of Team Free Will who wears an overcoat? Cas has become a true member of the Winchester family.

LIVE AND LET DIE

The Winchesters confront death about as often as they gas up the Impala: all the time. But dying is rarely the end of the road—it's usually more of a pit stop. Here's a look at our fave ways the brothers have (temporarily) shuffled off this mortal coil. **BY SAMANTHA HIGHFILL**

1 | DRAGGED TO HELL, PART 2

S5, E22

A death never felt more final than it did at the end of showrunner and creator Eric Kripke's five-season apocalyptic story arc. It's all about when Sam takes hold of Lucifer in his mind and willingly sacrifices his freedom to jump into Hell—specifically, the Cage.

2 | DRAGGED TO HELL

S3, E16

A year after Dean sells his soul to save Sam's life, it's time to pay up. No true fan will forget how they felt when the Hellhounds came calling for Dean.

3 | ANGELS ARE DICKS

S9, E23

Sam arrives just in time to see Metatron kill Dean, and as Sam holds his brother, Dean uses his final breath to tell Sam, "I'm proud of us." Tissues, please.

4 | STABBED IN THE BACK, LITERALLY

S2, E21

It's Sam's first death on the show—and, in fact, the first real death of either Winchester brother. When combined with Dean watching helplessly, it's downright unforgettable.

5 | A DEADLY FUTURE

S5, E4

The angel Zachariah gives Dean a grim glimpse of the future, which culminates when present-day Dean comes face-to-face with Lucifer-Sam, who snaps future Dean's neck.

6 | SO MANY DEATHS, SO LITTLE TIME

S3, E11

In "Mystery Spot," Sam finds himself stuck in a world where every day ends with Dean biting it in some crazy way. Most of the hour is played for laughs, but the episode was Padalecki's least favorite to film. "That was a miserable, miserable, miserable week in my life," he says. "I could only treat it like it was reality.... Sam would be mortified.... 'My brother is dead in my arms.'" The final death (Dean shot by a mugger) struck an unexpectedly dramatic tone and left viewers wondering if Dean would open his eyes again.

7 | SHOTGUN TO THE HEART

S5, E16

In two of the more violent demises, Sam and Dean were executed at close range in a motel room. In a show that's about the fantastic, the reality of death by gun only made it more shocking. The guys swiftly returned to the living after a memorable trip to Heaven.

8 | DEAD AND ALIVE AGAIN IN 60 SECONDS

S5, E13

Anna stabbed Sam in the stomach, but he was only down for a few minutes before Michael brought him back. Yet the scene carried weight, if only because of the panicked look on Dean's face as he watched his brother collapse. (Bonus points for the Michael-in-John-Winchester's-body twist.)

9 | AN UNWANTED VACATION

S7, E23

When Dick Roman finally died, he took Castiel and Dean with him...all the way to Purgatory, the effects of which would play out in the next season. However, in terms of the moment of death, it was almost too fast for viewers to feel anything.

10 | THE ULTIMATE SHOCK

S4, E8

Sam getting struck by lightning, while cool, doesn't quite register on an emotional level, both because it lasted all of three seconds and because it was mostly played for laughs.

6

4

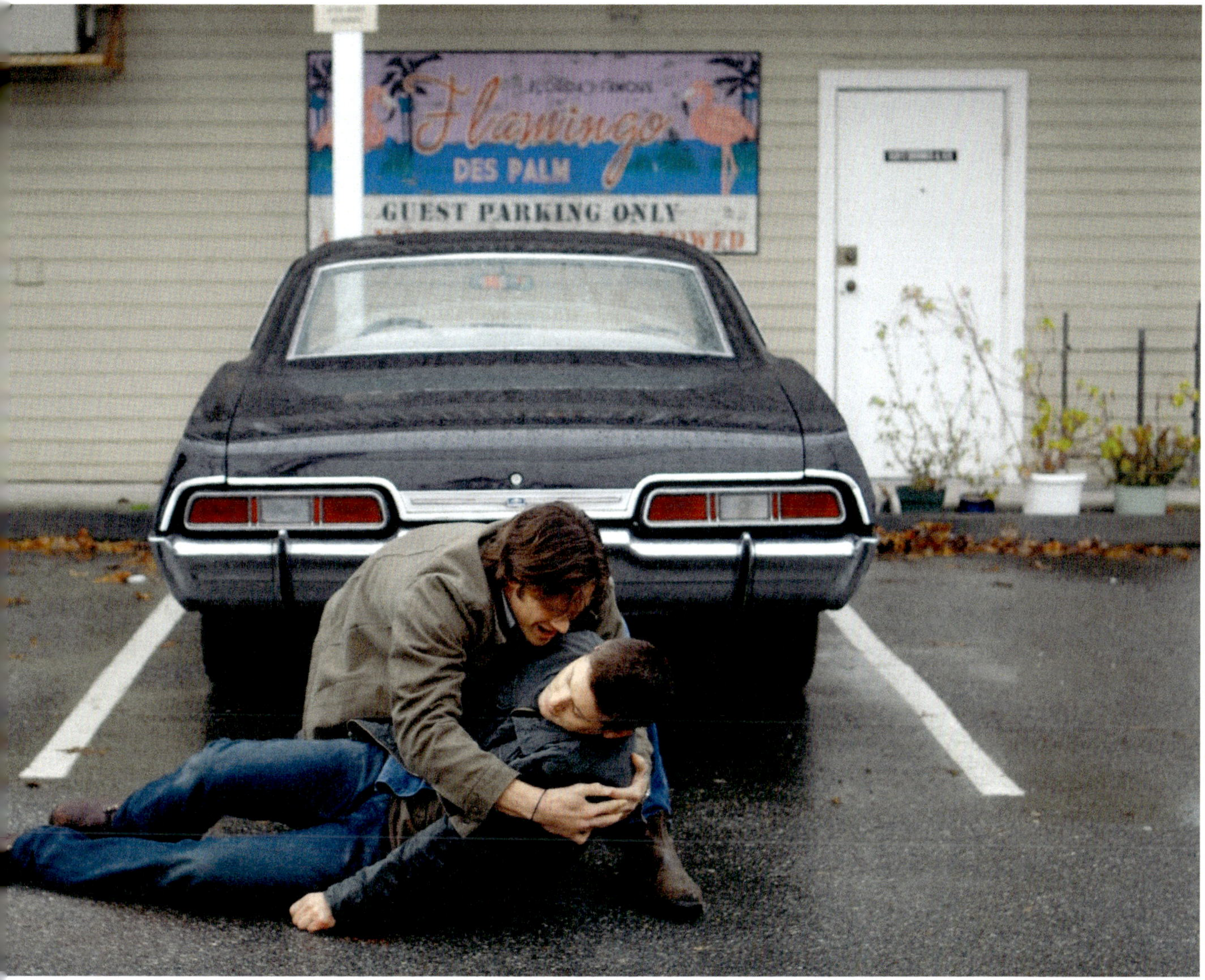
Flamingo
DES PALM
GUEST PARKING ONLY

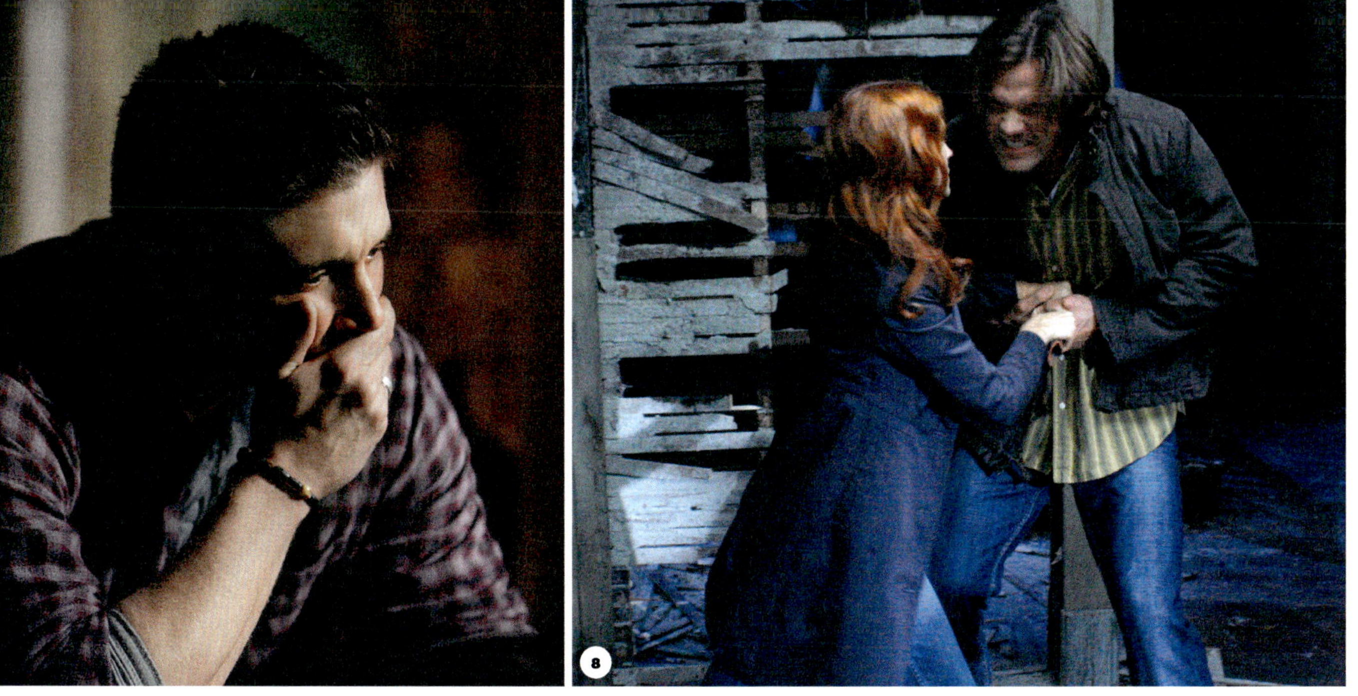

8

The Community
SUPERNATURAL

FANS AND CAST UNITE AS ONE #SPNFAMILY

ILLUSTRATION BY KAGAN McLEOD

FUNimation
MY HERO ACADEMIA
4300

Whole Lotta Love

WHEN HE ACCEPTED THE ROLE OF BOBBY SINGER, ACTOR JIM BEAVER HAD NO IDEA THAT A TV SHOW FEATURING MONSTERS, ANGELS AND DEMONS WOULD CHANGE HIS LIFE FOREVER. THE ACTOR SHARES HIS FIRST-PERSON TAKE ON JOINING THE *SUPERNATURAL* FAMILY

Fans crowd to see the *Supernatural* stars at Comic-Con International San Diego in 2017.

*His recurring character Bobby Singer started as a beloved father figure to the two Winchester boys. And when Jim Beaver first met Jensen Ackles and Jared Padalecki, he enjoyed an easy, immediate rapport with the two stars. "*Supernatural *is the happiest set I've ever worked on," Beaver said. But once he had a chance to interact with the show's devoted fans, he realized he'd accepted a role that would change his life.*

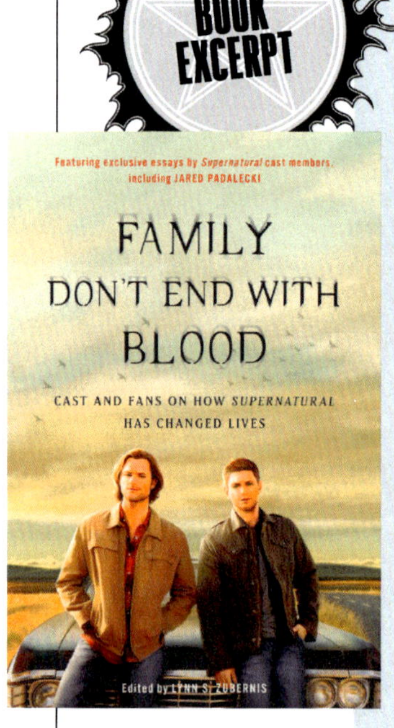

Excerpt from Family Don't End With Blood *by Jim Beaver and Lynn Zubernis. Copyright (c) 2017 by the author and reprinted by permission of BenBella Books, Inc.*

As we finished shooting season 3, I got my first invitation to a *Supernatural* convention. It was held in April 2008, in Orlando, Florida. The last fan convention I'd attended with my wife was in a small comic-book store in Bologna, Italy, and about twenty fans showed up. So I was utterly flabbergasted by the turnout in Orlando. For a guy who'd spent thirty-six years acting without anyone paying any particular attention, walking into the EyeCon ballroom felt like I'd been reincarnated as Elvis. It was extraordinary and very touching and gratifying.

In some ways, that first convention was also the most important I've attended, because it was there that I really learned who our audience was. First off, since the *Star Trek* events I'd gone to with Cecily were dominated by male fans, I was floored in Florida by the near-total absence of testosterone. I think I counted four or five men in attendance. For a long time, this gave me the impression that only women watched *Supernatural*. It took me a long time to figure out that, no, lots of men watch *Supernatural*. But mainly women attend the conventions. At least the numbers are overwhelmingly in their favor. (I don't mind. I don't mind at all.)

The warmth with which I was treated at that first convention, and at every subsequent one, startled me. I don't think I'd realized what a chord the character of Bobby had struck in the audience, nor was I prepared for the affection they showed the fellow who played him. The convention was small enough that I was able to mingle with the fans between events and to hang out for hours together in the evenings. That weekend I made friends who are still vital parts of my life—dear, treasured friends.

I also learned a lot about how the fans felt about the show. The most startling revelation was when someone told me that she watched the show mostly for the relationships, that she would watch *Supernatural* even if there weren't any monsters. It was said to me in a crowd and I asked, "Really?" Almost in unison, the crowd yelled, "Yes! Absolutely!".... I've been to dozens of fan conventions since 2008, and this impression has been reinforced at every such event.

The final real and lasting effect of *Supernatural* on my life, beyond the friendships and insights, has been the realization that through the vast community of fans of this show, I can have an enormous effect for good. Social media has been invaluable for this. A few years ago, one of the crew on *Supernatural* asked me to tweet something about the cancer charity he was supporting. Because I'd lost both my wife and my dear friend Kim Manners to the disease in recent years, I was more than willing to do whatever I could, and God knows a simple tweet was not hard to do. What shocked me was that within an hour or two of that tweet, the charity's tote board shot up thousands of dollars. I began to realize that I might not have been placed in this remarkable and wonderful position simply to do what I love (acting) and to meet adoring fans. Maybe I was here to make a difference, and to make that difference by helping the gigantic *Supernatural* fan base make a difference.

Since then, I've tried (judiciously) to bring the *Supernatural* Family (and that's what it is, a family) together to support things that seem worthy and helpful to the world.... To have any positive effect outside our own personal circles is a blessing few of us are allowed to achieve. I have done so only through the worldwide family of *Supernatural*.

It is difficult for me to overstate the effect being Bobby Singer has had on me. It has given me more visibility than I ever dreamed likely. It has given me a raft of friends (and even a romance or two) among my colleagues and fans of the show. It has allowed me to travel around the world (literally!) meeting people I'd never otherwise have learned about. It has made a rather shy and private person into someone who revels in the company of people he has never before met. It has made me feel appreciated and loved, not only for my work but also for myself, which is a pretty amazing accomplishment for even a few million people to pull off. And it has shown me that the vast weight of love and kindness and humanity in the world can and does overwhelm the forces of spite, hate, and ingratitude. The *Supernatural* effect on me has been the greatest gift of my public life. And anyone who doesn't think so is an idjit.

> “The *Supernatural* effect on me has been the greatest gift of my public life”
>
> –*Jim Beaver*

Clockwise from top left: Jim Beaver answering questions at Salt Lake Comic Con in 2016; Jared Padalecki signs at SDCC 2017; also at SDCC 2017, Jensen Ackles meets with a star-struck fan in 2017; Misha Collins in 2017.

SECOND BANANAS NO MORE

For fans, character actors Richard Speight Jr. and Rob Benedict are like Gods. To the rest of the world, they're just two performers working in L.A. That disparity inspired them to create their cult streaming series *Kings of Con*. **BY SAMANTHA HIGHFILL**

Benedict and Speight Jr. dress up, act out and welcome frequent *Supernatural* guest stars, such as Misha Collins (bottom left, with monkey) and Kurt Fuller (top, at far right).

STANDING ON STAGES AT *SUPERNATURAL* fan conventions all over the world, Rob Benedict and Richard Speight Jr. are superstars. After all, Benedict spontaneously recurs as God on the show, and Speight played Gabriel in early seasons before graduating to direct episodes. But the moment any given convention ends, the two are back to living everyday lives.

"One of the things that stood out to us in doing cons," says Speight, referring to conventions, "was the disparity between going into a hotel packed with people who are literally tripping over each other to get your autograph and then leaving that hotel on Sunday and coming back to a town where you are [unknown.] The juxtaposition is pretty dramatic."

That shift, combined with the strange encounters that occur with the passionate fans who frequent the con world, gave them an idea for a show of their own in early 2014. When they were asked to cohost some of the conventions—introducing panels and providing entertainment—they realized that they had their ideal opportunity. That's when they filmed the pilot for *Kings of Con*, a comedy-short series that tells the story of Rob and Rich, exaggerated versions of Benedict and Speight, who are "superfamous...13 weekends a year," according to the show's tagline.

The actors started an Indiegogo campaign, raising nearly $280,000 to film the show's first season, which was later picked up by Comic-Con HQ for a 10-episode slate (all episodes are now streaming).

Each episode of the Web series takes place in a different city, with other *Supernatural* stars frequently stopping by (the first season included appearances by Misha Collins, Jensen Ackles, Jared Padalecki and more). "They've all been incredibly supportive of it," says Benedict. "We all do this together. It's not just Rich and me."

Speight adds, "When you go to the hierarchy of the show, Rob and I were recurring characters. We were fortunate to have characters that made a big impact, but we weren't long-standing players on the show. But in the con world, we've all been there the same amount of time." He pauses and considers another way of putting it: "It's like we've basically been opening for the Rolling Stones on tour for the last seven years," he says with a laugh.

Although the show's first season gained a solid fan base, *Kings of Con* is now looking for a new home. But Speight and Benedict are confident it will find one. In fact, they've already started writing season 2. "We're going to do it," Speight says. "We've been crafting stories. We're just waiting to figure out where we're going to go."

COME TOGETHER

The stars of *Supernatural* are doing their best to live up to the Winchesters' reputation as heroes.

BY SAMANTHA HIGHFILL

AS FAR AS SAM AND DEAN WINCHESTER ARE concerned, saving people is quite literally their job. They wake up every day and try to figure out who they can help and how (which usually means figuring out which monster needs killing). With Castiel by their side, they head out to save the day—or the world, depending on the situation.

But outside of the *Supernatural* universe, actors Jared Padalecki, Jensen Ackles and Misha Collins, have, in various ways over the years, made every effort to help people in the real world.

In 2009 Collins got an idea that would evolve into Random Acts, a nonprofit organization through which he's been able to partner with other organizations to do a whole lot of good. For example, 2011 saw the launch of GISHWHES (The Greatest International Scavenger Hunt the World Has Ever Seen). People from more than 100 countries have participated in the annual event; the hunt has involved staging such activities as hosting tea parties at a children's hospital or finding homes for Syrian refugees. "I'm proud that this fandom has coalesced around this game that actually does some good things for people," Collins says. (Collins announced that 2017's would be the final GISHWHES "as we have known it," but he hopes "there will be a future iteration of GISHWHES—something wildly different, perhaps.")

Random Acts is also home to the Crisis Support Network, a community support system for the *Supernatural* family and others that was the brainchild of Collins, Ackles and Padalecki. In partnership with Pop Culture Hero Coalition, To Write Love on Her Arms and IMAlive, the Crisis Support Network is a place for *Supernatural* fans to come when they need help coping with mental-health issues. Fans can also volunteer with the network, which offers training to anyone who's interested. "I think one of the big problems that people face when they're struggling...is not knowing where to turn," Collins says. "But if you are part of a community and you know that community is offering help, it might be really helpful. That's what me and Jared and Jensen thought."

Additionally the stars have participated in charitable T-shirt campaigns with Represent.com. For example, Padalecki and Ackles have launched multiple variations of the "Always Keep Fighting" campaign, with proceeds going to a long list of charities, including To Write Love on Her Arms—a nonprofit dedicated to assisting those struggling with depression, addiction, self-injury and suicide—and the OneOrlando Fund, which offered financial aid to the families of and victims of the 2016 Pulse nightclub shooting.

"If we can help in any way, then I believe it's our duty as human beings and as people that are in a position to do so," Ackles says. "There are people out there that could use the help and encouragement, and those are the people we're trying to reach."

> "If we can help in any way, then I believe it's our duty as human beings...to do so"
>
> *–Jensen Ackles*

Clockwise from top left: Misha Collins working with Random Acts in Nicaragua; Jared Padalecki and Jensen Ackles showing off their T-shirts for charity; Collins in Haiti; Collins and crew break ground at the Free High School of San Juan del Sur in Nicaragua.

THE GREATEST SCAVENGER FINDS

The many teams that compete (for charity!) in the Greatest International Scavenger Hunt the World Has Ever Seen (GISHWHES) create art pieces, elaborate photos and more—often with a Supernatural *theme.*

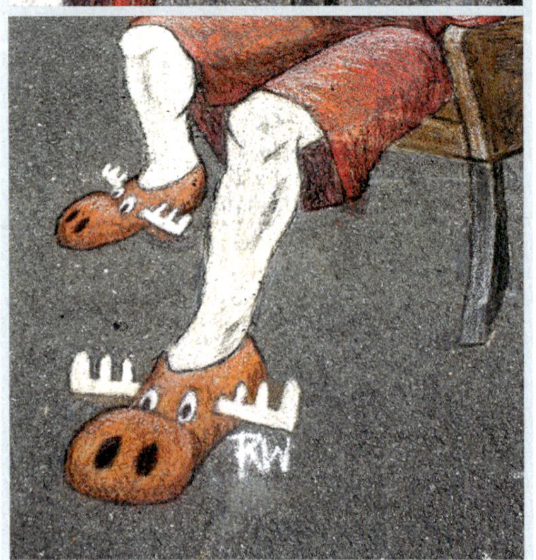

On left (from the 2014 challenge): a chalk portrait of *Supernatural* creator Eric Kripke, complete with Moose and Squirrel (Crowley's nickname for Sam and Dean). Above: a 2016 entry depicting various characters in the style of Picasso. Right: a portrait of Padalecki made entirely of Swedish Fish from the 2011 challenge. Far right: Jim Beaver's Bobby Singer, in cat fur.

Misha Collins (left) participating in the 2012 challenge of "Wear cheese and wear it well." (That's all cheese.) Below: a stained glass window portraying Castiel and the Impala.

"This little online scavenger hunt started as a lark, and now we have people from 100 different countries participating"

–Misha Collins

Carry On my Wayward Sons

FROM THE WOMAN IN WHITE TO SAM AND DEAN'S RECENT STINT IN PRISON, WE'VE RANKED EVERY SINGLE EPISODE OF *SUPERNATURAL* TO DATE. AND WE'RE PRETTY SURE IT WAS JUST AS DIFFICULT AS THAT ONE TIME THE WINCHESTERS STOPPED THE APOCALYPSE.

By Chancellor Agard, Jonathon Dornbush, Samantha Highfill

1 | SWAN SONG

S5, E22

It's the five-season finale creator Eric Kripke always imagined: the showdown between Lucifer (in Sam's body) and Michael, all set to Chuck's epic voiceover. After killing Cas and Bobby, Lucifer beats Dean to a pulp. It's Dean's love for Sammy that saves the day: when memories of the times the Winchesters spent together in the Impala come pouring back, Sam gets a grip on the devil and jumps into the Cage, one final sacrifice.

2 | THE FRENCH MISTAKE
S6, E15

It's time to get meta. The angel Balthazar throws Sam and Dean into an alternate reality where they play actors named Jared Padalecki and Jensen Ackles on the set of a show called *Supernatural.* Everything is up for a laugh: Sam has a wife ("You married fake Ruby?"), and Misha Collins can't stop tweeting.

3 | BABY
S11, E4

Told entirely from the perspective of the Impala, the show reminded fans of what it does best: brother bonding.

4 | LAZARUS RISING
S4, E1

Dean appears back on Earth having somehow escaped Hell, and things only get better when we discover how he got out. Castiel's entrance is still one of the best moments in the show's history.

5 | THE MONSTER AT THE END OF THIS BOOK
S4, E18

The Winchesters discover there's been a book series written about their exploits—with quite the online fandom (including strange and uncomfortable fan fiction). The author Chuck (Rob Benedict) is revealed as God's prophet.

6 | CHANGING CHANNELS
S5, E8

Thanks to the Trickster, Sam and Dean are trapped in a television world. Poking fun at the likes of *Grey's Anatomy* and Japanese game shows, it culminates in Sam's turning into

KITT from *Knight Rider.* Comedy aside, the episode also reveals that the Trickster is really the Archangel Gabriel.

7 | **ABANDON ALL HOPE . . .**
S5, E10

When Cas, Bobby, Ellen and Jo team up with Sam and Dean to take down Lucifer, things don't go as planned. In a heartbreaking death scene, Jo and Ellen sacrifice themselves to help get Sam and Dean in range of Lucifer...only to find out the Colt doesn't work on the devil.

8 | **LUCIFER RISING**
S4, E22

The revelation that some of Heaven's highest-ranking angels wanted the Apocalypse to happen came a little too late for the demon-blood-drinking Sam, who breaks the final seal and releases Lucifer from his Cage.

9 | **NO REST FOR THE WICKED**
S3, E16

Dean is dragged to Hell by a pack of Hellhounds; Sam and Bobby work to find a way to avoid his (inevitable) death.

10 | **THE END**
S5, E4

The angel Zachariah sends Dean five years into the future, where a demonic virus has taken over, and future Dean now leads a militia that includes an orgy-loving Castiel. In this world Sam said yes to Lucifer.

11 | **DARK SIDE OF THE MOON**
S5, E16

The boys visit Heaven. It's a brilliant way to handle the God question without actually introducing Him, while also hinting that this was not their first visit.

12 | **SACRIFICE**
S8, E23

Dean begs Sam to stop the third trial because, even though it will close the gates of Hell, it also will kill him. Bonus: an almost-human Crowley raving about HBO's *Girls*.

13 | **JUS IN BELLO**
S3, E12

The hunt for Bela turns into the show's coolest bottle episode.

14 | **ALL HELL BREAKS LOOSE: PT. 1**
S2, E21

Yellow Eyes sends Sam and all of his other "special" children into a *Hunger Games* scenario, culminating with Sam knifed in the back and dying in Dean's arms.

15 | **TWO MINUTES TO MIDNIGHT**
S5, E21

Dean meets with Death (Julian Richings) at a Chicago pizza joint.

16 | **THE BENDERS**
S1, E15

Sam is kidnapped by ordinary humans...who just happen to be homocidal psychopaths.

17 | **POINT OF NO RETURN**
S5, E18

Dean prepares to say yes to Michael. Cas gets so angry he beats Dean into unconsciousness in a scene that is as powerful as it is heart-wrenching. Finally poor Adam says yes instead.

18 | DEATH'S DOOR
S7, E10

All good things must come to an end. Bobby is dying, but what really sells his farewell is the episode's final scene as he relives a night shared with Sam and Dean, his memory of them fading away. The waiting Reaper gives him an ultimatum: cross over or remain as a ghost.

19 | MYSTERY SPOT
S3, E11

It's a twisted *Groundhog Day* for Sam, thanks to the Trickster: Every day ends with Dean's dying. By the end of the hour Dean has perished more than 100 times, and Sam just wants his brother back.

20 | NIGHTSHIFTER
S2, E12

The boys are trapped with a group of hostages and a shape-shifter inside a Milwaukee bank; the FBI believes they're robbers.

21 | ALL HELL BREAKS LOOSE, PT. 2
S2, E22

Yellow Eyes perishes; Dean sells his soul to bring back Sam; and the world's largest Devil's Trap is broken.

22 | GOOD GOD, Y'ALL!
S5, E2

War (Titus Welliver) guest stars, driving a wedge between Dean and Sam at a time when sticking together is key.

23 | HAMMER OF THE GODS
S5, E19

The Winchesters are trapped in a hotel full of gods (Kali, Odin and Ganesh, to name a few),

18

25

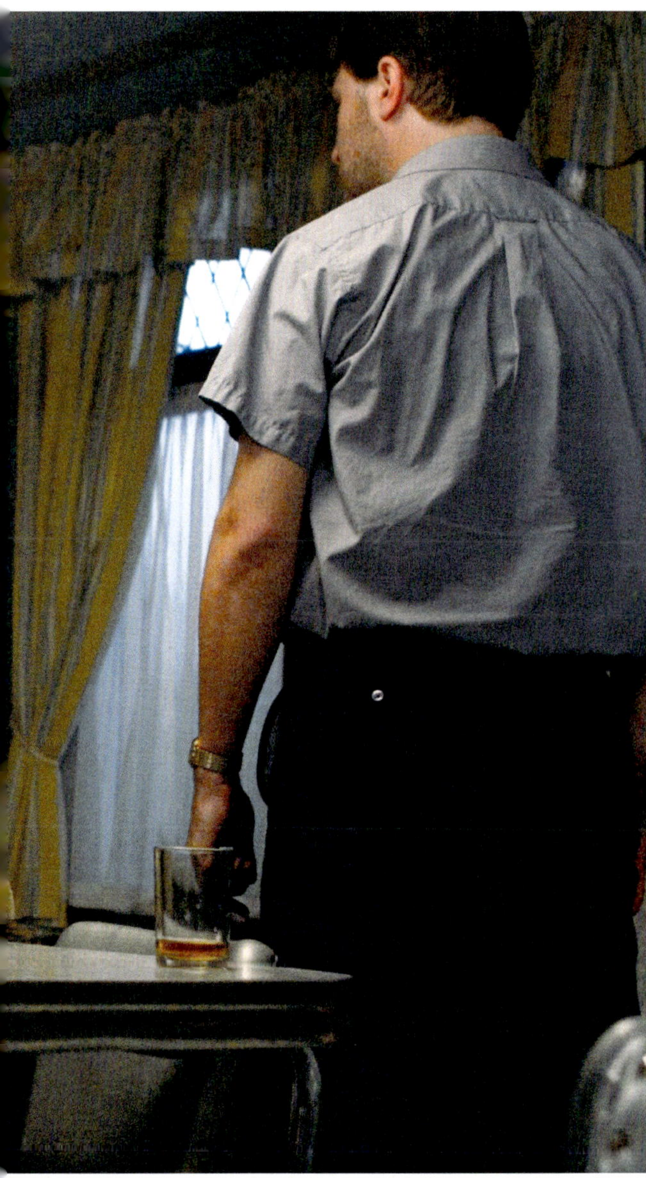

who are meeting to discuss what to do about the upcoming apocalypse.

24 | FREE TO BE YOU AND ME
S5, E3

Sam takes a break from hunting, and Dean and Cas search for Raphael.

25 | FAN FICTION
S10, E5

For the show's 200th episode, Sam and Dean visit an all-girls school, where they are putting on a musical version of Carver Edlund's *Supernatural* books. Our fave song: "A Single Man Tear."

26 | DON'T CALL ME SHURLEY
S11, E20

The author/prophet Chuck is definitively introduced as God, who summons Metatron for help in writing his autobiography.

27 | DEVIL'S TRAP
S1, E22

The brothers enlist the help of Bobby Singer (Jim Beaver), the man who will become their surrogate father and a staple on the show. Everything comes to a head when Yellow Eyes possesses John and Sam can't make himself shoot his father.

28 | IN MY TIME OF DYING
S2, E1

John sells his soul (oh, *and* the Colt) to Yellow Eyes to save Dean's life.

29 | 99 PROBLEMS
S5, E17

The boys are trapped by demons in a town run by the Whore of Babylon.

30 | PAC-MAN FEVER
S8, E20

Video-game logic rules in a Djinn-dream. Felicia Day guest-stars as Charlie.

31 | WHEN THE LEVEE BREAKS
S4, E21

Sam tries to demon detox but fails. The episode ends with a brother-on-brother brawl that leaves Dean bloodied on the floor of a hotel room.

32 | THE MAN WHO WOULD BE KING
S6, E20

The entire sixth season is retold from Castiel's (tragically shortsighted) perspective. We feel bad.

33 | JUST MY IMAGINATION
S11, E8

Sully, Sam's imaginary childhood friend, pops up to ask for help in solving a series of murders. Richard Speight Jr. (who played Gabriel) directs.

34 | HOLY TERROR
S9, E9

RIP, young Kevin Tran (Osric Chau).

35 | THE MAGNIFICENT SEVEN
S3, E1

The Seven Deadly Sins face off against a new Winchester ally: Ruby (Katie Cassidy).

36 | SYMPATHY FOR THE DEVIL
S5, E1

The boys think Cas is dead; Chuck can only tell them so much lest he incur angelic wrath, and Dean is told he's Archangel Michael's vessel. And there's still that one little problem: Lucifer found a host (Mark Pellegrino).

37 | **FIRST BORN**
S9, E11
Dean and Crowley team up to find the First Blade and run into the ridiculously charming Cain (Timothy Omundson). Dean walks away with the Mark of Cain on his arm.

38 | **THE SONG REMAINS THE SAME**
S5, E13
Angels travel back in time to kill John and Mary before Lucifer's host is born, and the Winchesters tag along to stop them.

39 | **THE MAN WHO KNEW TOO MUCH**
S6, E22
Sam's time without a soul finally comes back to haunt him. Meanwhile Castiel, drunk on Purgatory souls, declares himself the new God.

40 | **BORN UNDER A BAD SIGN**
S2, E14
Sam's possessed by Meg, who's back from Hell to torture Dean.

41 | **GHOSTFACERS**
S3, E13
When Sam and Dean meet the Ghostfacers for the second time, they've got their own reality show—*and* a theme song. Things get tricky when one of their own actually dies. Sorry, Corbett.

42 | **KING OF THE DAMNED**
S9, E21
The battle for the crown of Hell is finally decided with a little help from Dean, who impales Abaddon (Alaina Huffman) with the First Blade—and then mutilates her corpse.

43 | **DO YOU BELIEVE IN MIRACLES?**
S9, E23
Metatron is unstoppable in his quest to become the new God until his hubris is used against him. He mortally injures Dean, leaving Sam to mourn his brother (again). Then Dean wakes up with a pair of black demon eyes.

44 | **PILOT**
S1, E1
It's the hour that kicked off everything.

45 | **CROATOAN**
S2, E9
A demonic virus has taken over a town, and when Sam gets infected, classic brother moments ensue.

46 | **HEART**
S2, E17
Sam is forced to kill the woman he's falling for when she realizes she's a werewolf.

47 | **FIRST BLOOD**
S12, E9
Sam and Dean make a deadly deal with the Reaper Billie (Lisa Berry), but she's underestimated Castiel's attachment.

48 | **FAITH**
S1, E12
Sure, it ends up being about a Reaper, but with Dean's life hanging in the balance the episode packs an emotional punch.

49 | **THE DEVIL IN THE DETAILS**
S11, E10
Lucifer has manipulated Sam's dreams, and suddenly he's a player again. And Castiel says yes to being his vessel—but Sam and Dean don't know.

47

52

50 | **RED MEAT**

S11, E17

The boys are on a hunt, and Sam gets shot. It's a classic survivalist scenario unfolding at a slower-than-usual pace.

51 | **BROTHER'S KEEPER**

S10, E23

Death offers Dean a deal: He'll transport Dean far away to a place where the Mark of Cain won't affect the world anymore, but only if Dean kills Sam. For a moment it looks as if Dean is going to do it.

52 | **THE THINGS WE LEFT BEHIND**

S10, E9

Castiel's vessel was a man named Jimmy Novak, and he had a daughter, Claire (Kathryn Newton), who persuades Cas to break her out of a group home.

53 | **LARP AND THE REAL GIRL**

S8, E11

Not only does Charlie return, but Sam and Dean do a little LARPing.

54 | **HOLLYWOOD BABYLON**

S2, E18

The show's first real attempt at comedy lands Sam and Dean on a haunted film set with an obnoxious (and ill-fated) producer.

55 | **STAIRWAY TO HEAVEN**

S9, E22

Heaven's war is escalating, complete with suicide-bombing angels. A desperate Castiel calls on Sam and Dean for help.

56 | **MY BLOODY VALENTINE**

S5, E14

Sam uses his demon-blood powers to pull demon souls out of Famine and kill him. Also, Cas eats a lot of hamburgers.

57 | **IN THE BEGINNING**

S4, E3

Castiel sends Dean back in time to learn about his past. It's instructive: He helps John pick out the Impala, Azazel meets them for the first time, and Dean discovers the Campbells are hunters.

58 | **ON THE HEAD OF A PIN**

S4, E16

The angels ask for Dean's help as a torturer. The demon on the rack? His former master in Hell, Alastair himself.

59 | **O BROTHER WHERE ART THOU?**

S11, E9

While Sam is tormented by dreams of Lucifer, Dean fights his own strange attraction to Amara, the Darkness (Emily Swallow), caused by the Mark of Cain.

60 | **THE EXECUTIONER'S SONG**

S10, E14

It's the big battle between Dean and Cain and—spoiler alert!—Dean comes out victorious.

61 | **WHO ARE WE**

S12, E22

Mary Winchester has been brainwashed by the British Men of Letters. Meanwhile, the American hunters prepare to fight for their lives.

62 | **THE PRISONER**

S10, E22

Dean, under the influence of the Mark of Cain, rages when he discovers Charlie's murder.

41

63 | I KNOW WHAT YOU DID LAST SUMMER
S4, E9
The introduction of Anna (Julie McNiven) is matched with Sam finally telling Dean about his "connection" with the demon Ruby.

64 | GOODBYE STRANGER
S8, E17
While Castiel struggles through Naomi's mind control, the hunt is on for the demon tablet—and Meg lets it slip that there's an angel tablet too.

65 | THE REAL GHOSTBUSTERS
S5, E9
The Winchesters, in brilliant metafashion, attend a fan convention. Hi, Chuck!

66 | I THINK I'M GONNA LIKE IT HERE
S9, E1
All the angels have fallen from Heaven, and most of them are upset with Castiel. Meanwhile, Sam's in a coma as a result of the injuries he suffered during the trials, and the angel Ezekiel offers to help. Of course, there's a price.

67 | HEAVEN AND HELL
S4, E10
After a demon-and-angel showdown, Dean opens up about his time in Hell.

68 | WHAT IS AND WHAT SHOULD NEVER BE
S2, E20
Thanks to a Djinn, Dean lands in an alternate world where everything is wonderful. But while Mom's alive, the brothers aren't close, and it's a tearjerker when Dean has to say goodbye to Mary—and then wakes back up to his life on the road.

69 | ALL ALONG THE WATCHTOWER
S12, E23
Crowley sacrifices himself to trap Lucifer (and, accidentally, Mary) in an alternate dimension. Lucifer gets a last strike in and kills Castiel. Oh, and Lucifer's son is born.

70 | CLIP SHOW
S8, E22
Old characters return as part of a new case.

71 | LET IT BLEED
S6, E21
Dean's girlfriend Lisa (Cindy Sampson) and her son Ben (Nicholas Elia) are abducted by demons. It ends okay, but then Dean asks Cas to erase all their memories of him to help keep them safe.

72 | MOMMY DEAREST
S6, E19
Eve dies in a diner showdown. But the fight's far from over as Cas and Crowley meet up after all the bloodshed.

73 | ROAD TRIP
S9, E10
Crowley (who has a demon infiltrating the NSA?) has to possess Sam to save him from Gadreel.

74 | READING IS FUNDAMENTAL
S7, E21
Not only do we meet the tablets of God, but a new prophet is chosen: the soon-to-be-beloved Kevin Tran.

75 | THE BORN-AGAIN IDENTITY
S7, E17
Lucifer drives Sam into a mental hospital, and Dean uncovers Cas's new amnesiac identity.

90

76

78

81

76 | **MONSTER MOVIE**
S4, E5
Murders begin taking the form of classic horror films with mummies, werewolves and Dracula all to blame. It's a shapeshifter with a penchant for the Universal monsters who is the real foe.

77 | **FOLSOM PRISON BLUES**
S2, E19
The boys are thrown in jail, but that doesn't stop ghosts from popping up in their lives. At least Dean knows how to fit in after watching all those prison movies.

78 | **SAFE HOUSE**
S11, E16
Bobby and Rufus (Steven Williams) return in flashback as the boys hunt the same monster in present day.

79 | **ROCK NEVER DIES**
S12, E7
Cas, Crowley, Sam and Dean all work together to bring down Lucifer, who's currently living his best life as a rock star.

80 | **META FICTION**
S9, E18
Sitting at his typewriter, Metatron finally tells his side of the story in a wonderfully crafted hour.

81 | **MEET THE NEW BOSS**
S7, E1
Cas is God. Crowley's in hiding, with scotch.

82 | **YELLOW FEVER**
S4, E6
Dean gets a virus that makes him scared of just about anything, including very small dogs. It's a perfect balance of drama and comedy: Dean might die, and a cat might kill him.

83 | **WE HAPPY FEW**
S11, E22
It's the biblical battle we'd been waiting for: Chuck, Castiel and angels; Crowley and the demons; and Rowena and the witches—all versus Amara, a.k.a. the Darkness.

84 | **ALL IN THE FAMILY**
S11, E21
Chuck, the boys and Metatron attempt to rescue Lucifer, who is being tortured by Amara.

85 | **THE ONE YOU'VE BEEN WAITING FOR**
S12, E5
"Dean killed Hitler" is a sentence we'll never be tired of writing.

86 | **STUCK IN THE MIDDLE (WITH YOU)**
S12, E12
Mary invites her sons on a hunt but is double-crossed. A tense experiment in nonlinear storytelling.

87 | **INTO THE MYSTIC**
S11, E11
While hunting a banshee, the boys meet Eileen (Shoshannah Stern).

88 | **MY HEART WILL GO ON**
S6, E17
What if the *Titanic* never sank? More importantly, come on, Balthazar. What kind of angel could hate *Titanic*?

89 | **APPOINTMENT IN SAMARRA**
S6, E11
Death hands his powers over to Dean for a day.

90 | **TAXI DRIVER**
S8, E19
It's the second trial, and breaking into Hell apparently only requires a taxi-driving smuggler.

91 | **HOME**
S1, E9
Sam and Dean rid their family home of a poltergeist with help from the psychic Missouri (Loretta Devine) and ghost Mary.

92 | **A VERY SUPERNATURAL CHRISTMAS**
S3, E8
The brothers exchange Christmas gifts (the origins of the Samulet revealed!) and enjoy some quality family time—eggnog included.

93 | **THERE'S NO PLACE LIKE HOME**
S10, E11
Two different Charlies return from Oz.

94 | **ARE YOU THERE, GOD? IT'S ME, DEAN WINCHESTER**
S4, E2
Horror hits home as Bobby's place is overrun by ghosts and the brothers try to determine if Castiel is really an angel.

95 | **TRIAL AND ERROR**
S8, E14
The Winchesters hunt a Hellhound.

96 | **THE DEVIL YOU KNOW**
S5, E20
The truth behind Yellow Eyes' plans haunts Sam as he and Dean search for the final two Horsemen rings.

97 | **IT'S A TERRIBLE LIFE**
S4, E17
Zachariah sends Dean into a world where he's a corporate bro and Sam works in tech support.

98 | **FREAKS AND GEEKS**
S8, E18
A group of teenage misfits are hunting vampires.

99 | HUNTED
S2, E10
Sam investigates Yellow Eyes' "special children."

100 | THE GREAT ESCAPIST
S8, E21
Metatron's first appearance doesn't exactly hint at his later power grab; instead he helps the boys while Kevin tries to break free from Crowley.

101 | BOOK OF THE DAMNED
S10, E18
While Castiel and Metatron search for Cas's grace, Charlie and the boys try to translate the Book, which is in ancient Sumerian (and coded).

102 | REGARDING DEAN
S12, E11
Hit by a curse, Dean begins to lose his memory.

103 | SHADOW
S1, E16
The boys run into a familiar face: Meg, who uses them as bait to trap John.

104 | FORM AND VOID
S11, E2
When Sam is infected by the Darkness, we're introduced to Billie, a Reaper who has it out for the Winchesters.

105 | EVERYBODY LOVES A CLOWN
S2, E2
It's a smart mix of drama—John's funeral (or the closest thing to it)—and comedy. Plus, the boys meet Jo and Ellen Harvelle for the first time.

106 | NO EXIT
S2, E6
Jo joins as the boys hunt the ghost of an early serial killer: H.H. Holmes.

107 | FALLEN IDOLS
S5, E5
Sam wrestles with Gandhi before decapitating Paris Hilton. Thanks for this one, *Supernatural.*

108 | WE NEED TO TALK ABOUT KEVIN
S8, E1
Dean's back from Purgatory with a secret. He leaps back into the hunt, uncovering desperate messages from Kevin.

109 | I BELIEVE THE CHILDREN ARE OUR FUTURE
S5, E6
It's the introduction of Jesse, the anti-Christ. Whatever happened to him, anyway?

110 | SLUMBER PARTY
S9, E4
Charlie discovers Oz is a real place, and Dorothy is actually a kickass hero.

111 | WEEKEND AT BOBBY'S
S6, E4
It's just the average weekend where Bobby saves everyone's life and doesn't get a thank-you.

112 | CELEBRATING THE LIFE OF ASA FOX
S12, E6
Sheriff Jody Mills, Sam and Dean's surrogate mother meet the newly resurrected Mary Winchester at the funeral of a fallen hunter.

113 | ASK JEEVES
S10, E6
Sam and Dean work a case that oddly feels like a game of Clue.

114 | OUR LITTLE WORLD
S11, E6
Crowley attempts to control Amara for his own ends and fails.

111

130

135

127

115 | HELLO, CRUEL WORLD
S7, E2

The Leviathan of it all hurts this episode's credibility, but the return of Lucifer (in Sam's visions) almost makes up for it.

116 | DEVIL MAY CARE
S9, E2

Kevin is shocked when he realizes that Sam and Dean have kidnapped the King of Hell and shoved him into the trunk of the Impala.

117 | WHAT'S UP, TIGER MOMMY?
S8, E2

Who knew the supernatural world could be civilized enough to hold an auction? At various points, Crowley bids his soul (he doesn't have one); the *Mona Lisa* (the real one, where she's topless); and the moon.

118 | DEATH TAKES A HOLIDAY
S4, E15

Reapers aren't reaping; it's one of the 66 seals.

119 | SAM, INTERRUPTED
S5, E11

The boys go undercover at a psychiatric ward.

120 | BLOODY MARY
S1, E5

One of the series' scariest episodes tells the tale of Bloody Mary, who appears and makes people bleed from their eyes.

121 | THE VESSEL
S11, E14

Dean goes back in time to find a Hand of God.

122 | BITTEN
S8, E4

Sam and Dean stumble upon video footage that shows the werewolf transition of three college students...and the one of them who survives it all.

123 | SALVATION
S1, E21

Meg starts killing John's friends in order to get him to turn over the Colt.

124 | SOUL SURVIVOR
S10, E3

After a cat-and-mouse chase through the bunker, Sam saves his brother from being a demon.

125 | THE THIRD MAN
S6, E3

Castiel runs into an old angelic pal, Balthazar, who is stockpiling weapons that might be useful in the war with Raphael.

126 | DEAD MEN DON'T WEAR PLAID
S5, E15

Sheriff Jody Mills meets the boys, and unfortunately it's not under the best of circumstances: Her son's a zombie.

127 | HEAVEN CAN'T WAIT
S9, E6

The *Supernatural* writers make Cas human and force him to work at a gas station. Also, he babysits.

128 | BAD BOYS
S9, E7

Dylan Everett guest-stars as teenage Dean—and nails the mannerisms.

129 | AS TIME GOES BY
S8, E12

The Winchesters learn about their Men of Letters roots when their grandfather (guest Gil McKinney) time-travels to a motel room.

130 | HOOK MAN
S1, E7

A stellar example of the show's early days as a mini horror movie every week.

131 | JUMP THE SHARK
S4, E19

The episode lives up to its title, revealing that Sam and Dean aren't the only Winchester brothers. But the family reunion isn't exactly a fun time. Hello and goodbye, Adam.

132 | BLACK
S10, E1

Dean's a Knight of Hell, and Crowley is not finding him nearly as much fun (or useful) as he thought. In fact, much the opposite, and he keeps sticking Crowley with the tab.

133 | TALL TALES
S2, E15

The first appearance of the Trickster (Richard Speight Jr.) featured pranks aplenty, including a memorable alien abduction.

134 | THE CURIOUS CASE OF DEAN WINCHESTER
S5, E7

Dean turning into an old man thanks to a witchy poker game makes for a solid comedic hour that would've ranked much higher if the competition weren't so stiff.

135 | SCARECROW
S1, E11

The brothers are arguing, and Sam takes off for a bit. Thankfully, he comes back in time to save Dean from becoming the next sacrifice to a small town's pagan god.

136 | **HELL HOUSE**
S1, E17
The first appearance of the Ghostfacers isn't something we'll soon forget.

137 | **DON'T YOU FORGET ABOUT ME**
S11, E12
The Winchesters drop in on Jody Mills and her two adopted daughters.

138 | **DREAM A LITTLE DREAM OF ME**
S3, E10
When Bobby falls into a coma during a hunt, the boys rush to his side—and then into his dreams.

139 | **SOUTHERN COMFORT**
S8, E6
Garth (DJ Qualls) attempts to be the new Bobby, but the boys have concerns about a guy whose ringtone is "Jump" by Kris Kross in that role.

140 | **BEDTIME STORIES**
S3, E5
A spirit trapped inside a body hooked up to a life-support system begins haunting, using fairy tales as a vehicle.

141 | **AFTER-SCHOOL SPECIAL**
S4, E13
Going undercover as a gym teacher was a great idea, Dean. "The whistle makes me their god."

142 | **BAD DAY AT BLACK ROCK**
S3, E3
The boys meet Bela for the first time when she steals a (very) haunted rabbit's foot from Sam.

143 | **THE RAPTURE**
S4, E20
When Castiel is summoned back to Heaven, his human vessel tries to reclaim his family.

144 | **INSIDE MAN**
S10, E17
Sam and Castiel recruit the ghost of Bobby to break Metatron out of Heaven's prison.

145 | **LOTUS**
S12, E8
When Lucifer inhabits the body of POTUS, the boys have to ask the British Men of Letters for help. Also, Lucifer impregnates a woman, so there's *that*.

146 | **THE FOUNDRY**
S12, E3
Castiel and Crowley reluctantly team up to find and defeat Lucifer.

147 | **A LITTLE SLICE OF KEVIN**
S8, E7
Crowley is abducting future prophets to translate the angel tablet.

148 | **HUNTERI HEROICI**
S8, E8
There are enough retro animation callbacks in the episode, including an actual 1-ton anvil, that you can just sense Wile E. Coyote waiting offscreen for his cue.

149 | **SEASON 7, TIME FOR A WEDDING!**
S7, E8
Supernatural (you know, from those Edlund books) superfan Becky makes a deal with a demon and then gets hitched to Sam. Plus, we meet Garth.

150 | **SWAP MEAT**
S5, E12
Sam's body is stolen by a teenage boy.

158

146

149

141

151 | **FRONTIERLAND**

S6, E18

The boys go back in time to meet Samuel Colt, defeat a phoenix and reclaim the Colt.

152 | **EVERYONE HATES HITLER**

S8, E13

The title is great. The premise is great. The actual excitement of seeing a golem isn't what it could've been.

153 | **KEEP CALM AND CARRY ON**

S12, E1

Amara and Chuck are off reconnecting, Mary Winchester is resurrected (and is pretty suspicious about it), and a British Man of Letters abducts and tortures Sam.

154 | **OUT OF THE DARKNESS, INTO THE FIRE**

S11, E1

It's the official introduction of the Darkness, both as a full-grown woman and as a baby.

155 | **OF GRAVE IMPORTANCE**

S7, E19

Sam and Dean discover Bobby chose to remain on Earth as a ghost. In Dean's words, "What are the odds this ends well?"

156 | **TORN AND FRAYED**

S8, E10

Naomi's manipulation of Castiel starts to affect the ordinarily stoic angel.

157 | **REICHENBACH**

S10, E2

Crowley tries to control the newly demonized Dean and, when he gives up, sells him out to Sam. "There's the small matter of my finder's fee."

158 | **THE GIRL WITH THE DUNGEONS AND DRAGONS TATTOO**

S7, E20

If only Charlie's introduction weren't so entangled with all things Dick Roman, this episode would've ranked a lot higher.

159 | **THE GIRL NEXT DOOR**

S7, E3

Sam's softhearted nature comes back to haunt him when a monster he let go free as a child starts killing as an adult.

160 | **LIKE A VIRGIN**

S6, E12

Sam wakes up with his soul intact, and meanwhile, the brothers hunt a dragon.

161 | **ABOUT A BOY**

S10, E12

When Hansel gets his hands on Dean, the Winchester brother suddenly finds himself stuck in the body of his teenage self.

162 | **HELL'S ANGEL**

S11, E18

Lucifer makes an attempt at rallying Heaven behind him (yes, really) to defeat the Darkness. They aren't buying it.

163 | **#THINMAN**

S9, E15

It's not the most intriguing villain, but the parallels between Ed and Harry's relationship and Sam and Dean's are way too good to ignore.

164 | **LIVE FREE OR TWIHARD**

S6, E5

Supernatural takes a full-on shot at *Twilight*, showing the massive book-and-film franchise how exactly vampires are supposed to act.

165 | **ALPHA AND OMEGA**

S11, E23

The season 11 finale sees the resolution of God and Amara's conflict but introduces a new one: the British Men of Letters. Then there's the little matter of a resurrected Mary Winchester.

166 | **ROADKILL**

S2, E16

The boys help out a woman who has had a car accident. It's a slow reveal, but at the end she realizes she's a ghost.

167 | **THE FUTURE**

S12, E19

Sam decides on a path forward for Lucifer's unborn baby, but Castiel has other plans: He steals the Colt and goes after Dagon.

168 | **THERE'S SOMETHING ABOUT MARY**

S12, E21

The British Men of Letters declare war on the American hunters. First step: brainwashing and then weaponizing Mary Winchester to become their very own killing machine.

169 | **SIMON SAID**

S2, E5

Sam pursues another one of Yellow Eyes' special children and uncovers a man with the psychic ability of persuasion.

170 | **TIME AFTER TIME**

S7, E12

The God of Time sends Dean back to the 1940s, where he teams up with Eliot Ness, who just happens to be a hunter.

171 | **NIGHTMARE**
S1, E14
Sam's visions lead him to meet Max Miller, a man with telekinetic powers who lost his mother the same way Sam lost Mary.

172 | **MOTHER'S LITTLE HELPER**
S9, E17
Sam leaves Dean behind to work a case that mirrors one investigated by Henry Winchester and Josie Sands in 1958.

173 | **THE RAID**
S12, E14
Mary tries to recruit Sam and Dean to the British Men of Letters with a vampire hunt that goes wrong when the Alpha Vampire returns.

174 | **CAPTIVES**
S9, E14
Kevin is back, and he's haunting the bunker, at least until Sam and Dean find his mom.

175 | **LONG DISTANCE CALL**
S3, E14
Dean receives a call from his father—but it's really a crocotta.

176 | **SOMEWHERE BETWEEN HEAVEN AND HELL**
S12, E15
A rogue Hellhound causes Sam and Dean to team up with Crowley.

177 | **SOMETHING WICKED**
S1, E18
What is it with witches and stealing the life out of children?

178 | **CROSSROAD BLUES**
S2, E8
A local dive bar turns out to be the favorite hangout of a crossroads demon.

179 | **ADVENTURES IN BABYSITTING**
S7, E11
The introduction of Krissy (Madison McLaughlin) is a solid moment but not one of the most exciting.

180 | **THE MEMORY REMAINS**
S12, E18
What starts as an investigation into a man with a goat head ends up being a battle with the god Moloch—inside a freezer.

181 | **THIN LIZZIE**
S11, E5
It was only a matter of time until we ended up at Lizzie Borden's home.

182 | **HIBBING 911**
S10, E8
Jody Mills and Donna Hanscum bond at a sheriff's retreat (and the fandom goes wild!).

183 | **ASYLUM**
S1, E10
Sam and Dean rescue a couple from an abandoned sanitarium but not before they're turned against each other.

184 | **GIRLS, GIRLS, GIRLS**
S10, E7
Hannah is a big part of this hour when she discovers someone from her vessel's past.

185 | **THE USUAL SUSPECTS**
S2, E7
Sam and Dean struggle to solve a murder case when they end up in handcuffs.

186 | **IT'S THE GREAT PUMPKIN, SAM WINCHESTER**
S4, E7
Halloween turns deadly, and Uriel proves not all angels are alike.

221

187

189

187 | BLADE RUNNERS
S9, E16
Dean holds the First Blade in an hour that includes Snooki—as a crossroads demon, naturally.

188 | SEX AND VIOLENCE
S4, E14
This episode is also known as Sam and Dean meet a siren.

189 | THE KIDS ARE ALRIGHT
S3, E2
Lisa and Ben's first appearances are notable for obvious reasons, but let's not forget about all the creepy kids.

190 | REMEMBER THE TITANS
S8, E16
Sam and Dean try to help Prometheus by killing Zeus. Because sure, that sounds like an easy goal.

191 | AMERICAN NIGHTMARE
S12, E4
A devout family hide their daughter Magda in the basement.

192 | ROCK AND A HARD PLACE
S9, E8
The Winchesters wander through not-so-virgin territory and join a chastity group to investigate a series of murders. Dean struggles with the concept of chastity.

193 | THE WERTHER PROJECT
S10, E19
Sam asks Rowena to decode the codex for the Book of the Damned.

194 | ANGEL HEART
S10, E20
After Claire loses her mother, she's sent to live with Jody Mills.

195 | DEFENDING YOUR LIFE
S7, E4
Egyptian god Osiris puts Dean on trial.

196 | SHARP TEETH
S9, E12
Garth is back! But does he have to be a werewolf?

197 | SKIN
S1, E6
The first shape-shifter episode!

198 | MAMMA MIA
S12, E2
Mary Winchester teams up with Castiel and Dean to save Sam from the British Men of Letters.

199 | THE BAD SEED
S11, E3
Rowena is recruiting for a Mega Coven, and "Uncle Crowley" is trying to inspire Amara by showing her Hitler's speeches.

200 | LILY SUNDER HAS SOME REGRETS
S12, E10
After angels murdered her family, Lily Sunder has it out for Castiel.

201 | THE HUNTER GAMES
S10, E10
Sam and Dean interrogate Metatron about the Mark of Cain while Castiel bonds with Claire.

202 | I'M NO ANGEL
S9, E3
Three words: Castiel has sex. Okay, four: Twice.

203 | SLASH FICTION
S7, E6
Two Leviathans impersonate Sam and Dean and go on a killing spree that lands the brothers on the FBI's Most Wanted list.

204 | THE BRITISH INVASION
S12, E17
Mick Davies joins the Winchesters on the hunt for Kelly Kline.

205 | BEYOND THE MAT
S11, E15
If only we loved this episode as much as Dean loves wrestling.

206 | ...AND THEN THERE WERE NONE
S6, E16
We're not a huge fan of the worm-in-the-ear plot, and then we lose Rufus. RIP.

207 | SURVIVAL OF THE FITTEST
S7, E23
Dean and Cas go to Purgatory.

208 | CITIZEN FANG
S8, E9
Sam and Dean can't agree about Benny.

209 | THE THINGS THEY CARRIED
S10, E15
The Khan worm is back. This time it's after Cole.

210 | HALT & CATCH FIRE
S10, E13
Gotta love a vengeful ghost who uses electronic devices as a weapon.

211 | DOG DEAN AFTERNOON
S9, E5
Dean acting like a dog is funny on some levels—on others, less so.

212 | TWIGS & TWINE & TASHA BANES
S12, E20
Sam and Dean attempt to help Alicia and Max Banes find their mom.

213 | THE CHITTERS
S11, E19
The boys meet a pair of hunters with a personal connection to mysterious disappearances.

214 | PARTY ON, GARTH
S7, E18
The one with the shojo, a monster you can see only when you're drunk.

215 | FAMILY FEUD
S12, E13
Crowley's son Gavin goes back in time to save lives.

216 | RED SKY AT MORNING
S3, E6
How are people drowning when they're nowhere near water?

217 | FRESH BLOOD
S3, E7
Sam kills Gordon when he nearly bites Dean.

218 | EXILE ON MAIN ST.
S6, E1
The season 6 premiere introduces soulless Sam.

219 | TWO AND A HALF MEN
S6, E2
Sam needs Dean's help investigating missing babies.

220 | PAPER MOON
S10, E4
Werewolf attacks lead Sam and Dean to a familiar face: Kate (Brit Sheridan).

221 | THE PURGE
S9, E13
Sam as a yoga instructor is an image we'll never forget. Apart from the introduction of Donna, the episode is slightly less memorable.

222 | METAMORPHOSIS
S4, E4
The boys disagree on how to handle a rugaru.

Ranking All the Episodes

223 | **PROVENANCE**
S1, E19
That awkward moment when a family painting starts murdering its owners.

224 | **PLUSH**
S11, E7
Sheriff Donna calls Sam and Dean when a man in a giant fuzzy mask commits murder. (What else was she going to do?)

225 | **CRISS ANGEL IS A DOUCHE BAG**
S4, E12
The magicians certainly make for an entertaining hour, but not one we feel the need to rewatch.

226 | **DEAD IN THE WATER**
S1, E3
What first look like drowning deaths turn out to be the work of a vengeful spirit.

227 | **DARK DYNASTY**
S10, E21
A lot happens in this hour, but fans will always remember it as the one where Charlie dies.

228 | **LOVE HURTS**
S11, E13
This Valentine's Day episode can be summed up with one phrase: Kiss me *and* kill me.

229 | **WISHFUL THINKING**
S4, E8
Sam and Dean encounter a talking teddy bear. That's really all you need to know.

230 | **BLOOD BROTHER**
S8, E5
Dean's off to help Benny find his maker, leaving Sam to reflect on the life he had with Amelia.

231 | **FAMILY MATTERS**
S6, E7
Castiel finally realizes that Sam is missing his soul, which causes Dean to be even more skeptical of Samuel.

232 | **LADIES DRINK FREE**
S12, E16
After Claire is attacked by a werewolf, Sam and Dean work with Mick to save her life.

233 | **YOU CAN'T HANDLE THE TRUTH**
S6, E6
The goddess of truth gets Sam to admit he hasn't felt like himself since returning from the Cage. (Hint: He doesn't have a soul.)

234 | **REPO MAN**
S7, E15
The Winchesters face a demon they exorcised four years ago. Can anything just stay dead?

235 | **MALLEUS MALEFICARUM**
S3, E9
Witches, man. You don't want to mess with them.

236 | **PHANTOM TRAVELER**
S1, E4
A plane-crashing demon is a fine twist but nothing particularly notable.

237 | **PAINT IT BLACK**
S10, E16
A series of violent acts brings the boys to one specific Catholic church.

238 | **CAGED HEAT**
S6, E10
Sam and Dean work with Meg so that both parties can get the information they need out of the knowledgeable Crowley.

236

234

240

239 | **BLOODLUST**
S2, E3
What could be another vampire episode turns into the introduction of Gordon, a fellow hunter who's easy to love (despite turning down working with Sam and Dean at first).

240 | **HOW TO WIN FRIENDS AND INFLUENCE MONSTERS**
S7, E9
Not only does Dick shoot Bobby, but there's that unfortunate turducken thing, which—warning—will seriously mess with your appetite.

241 | **DEAD MAN'S BLOOD**
S1, E20
John reunites with his boys to investigate the death of a fellow hunter (and decapitate some vamps). You know, father-son stuff.

242 | **THERE WILL BE BLOOD**
S7, E22
The boys are in search of the three key items needed to defeat the Leviathan.

243 | **ALEX ANNIE ALEXIS ANN**
S9, E19
Jody Mills saves Alex (Katherine Ramdeen) from her vampire "family" and welcomes her into her own.

244 | **HOUSES OF THE HOLY**
S2, E13
What appears at first glance to be the introduction of angels to the show ends up being yet another vengeful spirit, though the experience does have the boys pondering the existence of God.

245 | **SIN CITY**
S3, E4
An investigation takes the Winchester boys to a town filled with gamblers and drinkers. No, it's not Las Vegas.

246 | **TIME IS ON MY SIDE**
S3, E15
We might have been able to live without the creepy Frankenstein-like doctor, but at least we're introduced to recurring badass Rufus.

247 | **HEARTACHE**
S8, E3
The case of the week is about a string of murders where all the suspects received organs from the same donor.

248 | **CHILDREN SHOULDN'T PLAY WITH DEAD THINGS**
S2, E4
Remember the college student with the zombie girlfriend? We only sort of do.

249 | **PLAYTHINGS**
S2, E11
A child's imaginary friend ends up being a ghost, because that's not scary or anything.

250 | **FAMILY REMAINS**
S4, E11
When a family moves into a haunted house, Sam and Dean have to show up and save the day. (Fun fact: *13 Reasons Why* star Dylan Minnette guest stars!)

251 | **SHUT UP, DR. PHIL**
S7, E5
Not even a *Buffy the Vampire Slayer* reunion can save this ho-hum episode about witches. It's a great title, though.

252 | **MAN'S BEST FRIEND WITH BENEFITS**
S8, E15
When an old friend starts having visions of killing people, Sam and Dean meet Portia, his familiar. What's a familiar? Just a witch's companion who can go back and forth between her human form and her animal one.

253 | **PLUCKY PENNYWHISTLE'S MAGICAL MENAGERIE**
S7, E14
Nothing good can come of a case that involves children's birthday parties, especially if you, like Sam, are afraid of clowns.

254 | **UNFORGIVEN**
S6, E13
This hour doesn't do much to move the overall plot forward; Sam and Dean go up against a less-than-exciting spiderlike foe.

255 | **BLOODLINES**
S9, E20
The back-door pilot to a potential spinoff about monster families in Chicago didn't quite live up to expectations. Needless to say, there was no spinoff.

256 | **THE MENTALISTS**
S7, E7
The most psychic town in American sounds fun, but the episode isn't much worth remembering.

257 | **THE SLICE GIRLS**
S7, E13
Dean sleeps with an Amazon warrior, she has a child, and then Sam has to kill the child before it gets Dean. Talk about bad decision-making, Dean.

258 | **ROUTE 666**
S1, E13
There's a haunted truck. Any questions?

259 | **MANNEQUIN 3: THE RECKONING**
S6, E14
When Dean heads off to handle a situation with Ben and Lisa—Lisa's dating—Sam is left to deal with mannequin hauntings. No thanks.

260 | **ALL DOGS GO TO HEAVEN**
S6, E8
This episode will make any dog lover wary of adopting a new pet for fear it might be a murderous skinwalker.

261 | **OUT WITH THE OLD**
S7, E16
This hour deals with Dick Roman and a cursed pair of ballet slippers that make people dance themselves to death.

262 | **CLAP YOUR HANDS IF YOU BELIEVE**
S6, E9
Dean is abducted by aliens that turn out to be fairies.

263 | **WENDIGO**
S1, E2
Coming off a strong pilot, episode 2 falls flat when the brothers take on a wendigo. Even creator Eric Kripke has admitted it's a weak hour.

264 | **BUGS**
S1, E8
Nothing works when a Native American curse is behind a deadly bug problem. Even the show's writers know how bad "Bugs" is—they've mocked it multiple times on the series.

SPECIAL THANKS
Brad Beatson, Melissa Frankenberry, Kristina Jutzi, Simon Keeble, Seniqua Koger, Kate Roncinske, Kristen Zwicker

Published by Time Inc. Books
225 Liberty Street
New York, NY 10281

We welcome your comments and suggestions about Entertainment Weekly Books. Please write to us at: Entertainment Weekly Books, Attention: Book Editors, P.O. Box 62310, Tampa, FL 33662-2310
If you would like to order any of our hardcover Collector's Edition books, please call us at 800-327-6388, Monday through Friday, 7 a.m.–9 p.m. Central Time.

PHOTO CREDITS
COVER: Frank Ockenfels 3/The CW; background: James Harris/EyeEm/Getty Images; **BACK COVER:** Matthias Clamer; **Pg 1:** Matthias Clamer; **Pg 2-3:** Matthias Clamer; **Pg 4:** Courtesy S.E. Hinton (2); **Pg 5:** Slash Fiction: Jack Rowand/The CW; Hinton and cast: Courtesy S.E.Hinton; Hinton: Stephen Holman/The NY Times/Redux; **Pg 6-7:** Kagan McLeod; **Pg 8-9:** Dean Buscher/The CW; **Pg 10-11:** Calvert, Ackles and Padalecki: Jack Rowand/The CW; Scooby-Win!: The CW; Padalecki and Calvert: Dean Buscher/The CW; **Pg 12-13:** Smith and Pellegrino: Jack Rowand/The CW; Castiel: Funko; Baby: Warner Bros.; book: Insight Editions (2); **Pg 14-15:** Collins: James Dittiger; Ackles: Sergei Bachlakov/The CW; **Pg 16-17:** group: Warner Bros. Television Entertainment; Speight: Bettina Strauss/The CW; **Pg 18:** Collins, Ackles, crew: Cate Cameron/The CW; Sheppard and Ackles: Katie Yu/The CW; **Pg 19:** James Dittiger; **Pg 20-21:** Matthias Clamer; **Pg 22-23:** Matthias Clamer (3); **Pg 24-25:** Matthias Clamer; **Pg 26-27:** Matthias Clamer; **Pg 28-29:** Kagan McLeod; **Pg 30-31:** Sergei Bachlakov/The CW; **Pg 32-33:** Sergei Bachlakov/The CW (4); Roadhouse group: David Gray/The CW; **Pg 34-35:** garage group, Armstrong, Rhodes and Smith: Diyah Pera/The CW (3); Swallow: Katie Yu/The CW; Omundson: Liane Hentscher/The CW; Pellegrino: David Gray/The CW; Richings: Jack Rowand/The CW; **Pg 36-37:** Frank Ockenfels 3/The CW; **Pg 38-39:** Padalecki and Ackles: Michael Muller/The CW; Gumenick, Morgan, Abel: Sergei Bachlakov/The CW (3); Smith: Katie Yu/The CW; Cohen: David Gray/The CW; **Pg 40-41:** James Dittiger (3); Devil's Trap: Sergei Bachlakov/The CW; **Pg 42-43:** Chuck Hodes/The CW;**Pg 44-45:** Ackles, Padalecki: Dean Buscher/The CW; Ackles and Cohen: Sergei Bachlakov/The CW; group: Katie Yu/The CW; under the hood: Tim Leong; **Pg 46-47:** Wallace: Liane Hentscher/The CW; Springfield: Bettina Strauss/The CW; **Pg 48-49:** Cole, Benz, McNab: Sergei Bachlakov/The CW (3); Bostwick, Blair: Michael Courtney/The CW (2); Hilton, Marsters and Carpenter: Jack Rowand/The CW (2); Polizzi: Katie Yu/The CW; **Pg 50-51:** Michael Courtney/The CW; **Pg 52-53:** Heyerdahl, Cassidy: Sergei Bachlakov/The CW (2); Padalecki, Sheppard: Diyah Pera/The CW; Miner: Jack Rowand/The CW; **Pg 54-55:** Miner: David Gray/The CW; Aycox, Cortese, Cassidy, Rolston: Sergei Bachlakov/The CW (4); Pellegrino, Boecher: Michael Courtney/The CW (2); Omundson, Sheppard: Diyah Pera/The CW (2); **Pg 56-57:** The CW; **Pg 58-59:** Ackles, Beaver and Collins: Jack Rowand/The CW; Chau: Diyah Pera/The CW; Benedict, Armstrong: Katie Yu/The CW; **Pg 60-61:** Cohen: Sergei Bachlakov/The CW; Speight, Fuller: Michael Courtney/The CW (2); Benedict: Bettina Strauss/The CW; Armstrong: Diyah Pera/The CW; Tapping: Liane Hentscher/The CW; Ware, Penikett, Collins: Jack Rowand/The CW (3); **Pg 62-63:** 6: Sergei Bachlakov/The CW; 4: Michael Courtney/The CW; 8: David Gray/The CW; **Pg 64-65:** Kagan McLeod; **Pg 66-67:** Warner Bros. Entertainment Inc.; **Pg 69:** Beaver: Stephan Starnes; Padalecki: Warner Bros. Entertainment Inc.; Ackles, Collins: Movie TV Tech Geeks (2); **Pg 70:** Comic-Con HQ (3); **Pg 71:** Temma Hopkins/Comic-Con HQ; **Pg 72-73:** Collins: Courtesy Random Acts (3); Padalecki: Courtesy Jared Padalecki (2); **Pg 74-75:** Courtesy GISHWHES; **Pg 76-77:** Jack Rowand/The CW; **Pg 78-79:** 15: Jack Rowand/The CW; 5: Sergei Bachlakov/The CW; 12: Diyah Pera/The CW; **Pg 80-81:** 18: Michael Courtney/The CW; 25: Diyah Pera/The CW; 27: Sergei Bachlakov/The CW; **Pg 82-83:** 47: Dean Buscher/The CW; 52: Liane Hentscher/The CW; 41: Sergei Bachlakov/The CW; **Pg 84-85:** 90,78: Diyah Pera/The CW (2); 76: Sergei Bachlakov/The CW; 81: Jack Rowand/The CW; **Pg 86-87:** 111: Jack Rowand/The CW; 127: Michael Courtney/The CW; 130,135: Sergei Bachlakov/The CW (2); **Pg 88-89:** 158: Jack Rowand/The CW; 146: Dean Buscher/The CW; 141,149: Michael Courtney/The CW (2); **Pg 90:** 221,187: Diyah Pera/The CW (2); 189: Sergei Bachlakov/The CW; **Pg 92:** 236: Sergei Bachlakov/The CW; 234,240: Jack Rowand/The CW (2); **Pg 94-95:** Matthias Clamer; **Pg 96:** 1,4,9: Sergei Bachlakov/The CW (3); 2,3,6,8: Diyah Pera/The CW (4); 5,7,10: Jack Rowand/The CW (3); 11: Michael Courtney/The CW; 12: Cate Cameron/The CW

Jared Padalecki and Jensen Ackles with Baby One.

SAM'S GOOD-HAIR DAYS

Only a dedicated fan could identify the ever-changing hairstyles of the younger Winchester brother. Can you match the correct Sam to the episodes below? Take some time to admire all the plaid.

A. **DEAD IN THE WATER**
S1, E3

B. **BORN UNDER A BAD SIGN**
S2, E14

C. **NO REST FOR THE WICKED**
S3, E16

D. **THE MONSTER AT THE END OF THIS BOOK**
S4, E18

E. **ABANDON ALL HOPE...**
S5, E10

F. **TWO AND A HALF MEN**
S6, E2

G. **OF GRAVE IMPORTANCE**
S7, E19

H. **TRIAL AND ERROR**
S8, E14

I. **MOTHER'S LITTLE HELPER**
S9, E17

J. **HALT & CATCH FIRE**
S10, E13

K. **LOVE HURTS**
S11, E13

L. **LILY SUNDER HAS SOME REGRETS**
S12, E10

A9; B4; C1; D11; E5; F7; G10; H3; I12; J2; K6; L8

51428056R00055

Made in the USA
Middletown, DE
11 November 2017